iPad Air 6th Generation User Guide

The Comprehensive Step-by-Step Instruction and Illustrated Manual for Beginners & Seniors to Master the 2024 iPad Air 6 (M2 Chip) with Tips and Tricks for iPadOS

Shawn Blaine

Copyright © 2024 by Shawn Blaine - All rights reserved.

This book is copyrighted, and no part may be reproduced, or transmitted via any means, be it electronic, internet, mechanical, or otherwise without the consent of the publisher except in a brief quotation or review of the book.

Table of Contents

Introduction 1
Chapter One 3
Set up iPad 3
Turn on your iPad 5
Set up Cellular Service 5
    Set up eSIM 5
Open Apps 6
Install New iPadOS 8
    Install iPadOS Automatically 9
    Install iPadOS Manually 9
Create your Apple ID 10
Chapter Two 11
Backup your iPad 11
    Enable iCloud Backup 11
    Manually Backup the iPad 11
    Backup with MacBook 12
    Back up with Windows Computer 12
Factory Reset the iPad 13
Chapter Three 14
Set up Apple Pay 14
    Add a Card for Apple Pay 14
    Adjust your Apple Pay Default Card 15
    Delete your Card 15

Set up Apple Cash 16
   Add Money to Apple Cash Card 16
   Send & Receive Funds 18
   Verify your Apple Pay Identity 20
Chapter Four 22
Set up Family Sharing 22
   Set up a Family Sharing Group 22
   Add a Family Member 22
   Set up an Apple ID for your Kid 23
   Delete a Member 23
   Exit a Family Sharing Group 23
Chapter Five 25
How to use Touch ID 25
   Add Touch ID 25
   Add Fingerprints Name 26
   Remove a Fingerprint 27
   Disable Touch ID 27
   Unlock the iPad with Touch ID 27
Set a Passcode 28
   Set the Passcode 28
   Adjust Automatic Lock 28
   Delete Data after 10 Failed Passcodes 29
   Disable the Passcode 30
Chapter Six 32
Add your Mail, Calendars & Contacts 32

Add Google Account 32
Add Outlook.com Account 32
Add Exchange Mail Account 33
Add Default Email Account....................... 34
Remove Email Account 34
How to use Hide My Email 34
Add Hide My Email Address 35
View Apps that use Hide My Email Address
.... 35
Disable Forwarding for a Hide My Email Address 36
Personalize the Hide My Email Forwarding Address 37
Chapter Seven.. 38
Connect Apple Pencil to iPad........................ 38
Pair the Apple Pencil 38
Disconnect the Apple Pencil...................... 38
View the Apple Pencil Battery 39
Charge the Apple Pencil 39
Chapter Eight 41
How to use AirDrop 41
Send an Item...41
Enable others to send Files to your iPad.....41
Disable Cellular Data for AirDrop.............. 42
Change AirDrop settings 42
Accept AirDrop 43

Chapter Nine 44

How to use the Control Center 44

    Open the Control Center 44

    Customize the Control Center 45

    Organize the Control Center 46

    Temporarily Disable a Wi-Fi 46

    Temporarily Disable Bluetooth 46

    Disable Access to Control Center in Apps .. 47

    Open Additional Controls in Control Center
.... 47

Chapter Ten 48

How to use Quick Note 48

    Open Quick Note 48

    Add Links to Quick Note 49

        Create a Link when you Create a Quick
        Note 49

        Create a Link via Text in Quick Note 50

    Delete a Quick Note 51

    Share a Quick Note 51

    Print a Quick Note 51

Chapter Eleven 52

How to use Stage Manager 52

    Enable Stage Manager 52

    Multitasking with Multiple Windows 54

    Switch between Apps 56

    Hide/Show the Recent Apps List 56

Close a Window 57

Transfer an App to an External Monitor 57

How to use Picture in Picture 58

Chapter Twelve 60

How to use Slide Over window 60

Open an App in Slide Over 60

Switch between Apps 61

Move the Slide Over window 61

Change Slide Over to Split View 62

Open a File in the Middle of the Screen 62

How to use Split View 63

Open a Second App in Split View 63

Replace an App 64

Chapter Thirteen 65

How to use Universal Control 65

Enable Universal Control on Mac 65

Enable Universal Control on iPad 66

Connect your Devices 67

How to use iPad as Second Monitor 67

Chapter Fourteen 69

How to use Siri 69

Enable Siri 69

Disable Siri 69

Change Siri's Language 70

Change Siri's Voice 70

- Chapter Fifteen 71
- How to use Widgets 71
  - Add Widget to Home Screen 71
  - Add Widgets in Today View 71
  - Remove Widgets from Today's View 72
  - Stack Widgets 72
  - Personalize a Stack Widget 73
  - Personalize your Widgets 73
- Chapter Sixteen 74
- How to Reorder Apps 74
  - Enable Edit Mode 74
  - Reorder Apps 74
  - Move Apps across Pages 75
  - Remove Apps from Home Screen 75
  - Create a Home Screen Folder for Apps 76
  - Rename Home Screen Folders 76
  - Transfer App from Folder to the Home Screen 77
  - Delete a Folder 77
- Reset the Home Screen & Apps 78
- Chapter Seventeen 79
- How to use FaceTime 79
  - Make FaceTime Call 79
  - Create a FaceTime Call Link 79
  - Delete a FaceTime Call Link 80
  - Use SharePlay in FaceTime 80

Turn on SharePlay 80

Use SharePlay to Play Music 81

Use SharePlay to Stream Videos 82

Turn on Portrait Mode for FaceTime 82

Turn on Voice Isolation 84

Turn on Wide Spectrum 84

Enable Center Stage 84

Chapter Eighteen 86

How to use Focus Mode 86

Enable a Focus Mode.................................. 86

Share your Focus Status 87

Allow Calls from Emergency Contacts 88

Sync your Focus settings 88

Add a Custom Focus 88

Remove a Focus 89

Chapter Nineteen 90

How to use the Camera App........................... 90

Capture a Photo 90

Turn on the Camera Flash.......................... 90

Zoom in or out 91

Capture a Panorama Image........................ 91

Capture a Live Photo 91

Capture with Burst mode 92

Take a Selfie 92

Mirror your Front Camera 93

Scan QR Code with Camera 93

Scan QR Code with Code Scanner 93

Capture a selfie in Portrait Mode 94

Adjust the Portrait Lighting Effect 94

Change Depth Control for Portrait Mode Selfies 95

Capture in Slow-motion 95

Shoot a Time-Lapse Video 95

Save Camera Settings 96

Enable Photo Grid 96

Change the Focus & Exposure 96

Personalize your Cinematic Mode Videos 97

Disable the Cinematic effect 97

Adjust the Focus Subject in a Cinematic Video 98

Change the Cinematic mode Depth of Field 98

Take a Screen Recording 99

Take a Screenshot 100

Chapter Twenty 101

How to use Live Text 101

Enable Live Text 101

Use Live Text with Camera 101

Disable Live Text for Camera 102

Translate, Copy and Look Up Text in an Image or Video 102

Perform Tasks on an Image or Video 103
Identify Objects with Visual Look Up 104
How to use the Document Scanner 104
Scan a Document 104
Share the Scanned Document 105
Remove a Scanned Document 106
Chapter Twenty-One 107
How to use Find My App 107
Adding iPad to Find My 107
Add Friends 107
Locate your Friends 108
Share your Location 108
Receive Alerts when your Friend Arrives or Exits a Location 109
Receive Alert when your Friend is not at a Location 110
Manage your Notification 110
Alert a friend when you Change Location .. 111
View all your Notifications 112
Disable Notifications about you 112
Locate Devices 113
Find Lost Devices 113
Erase a Device 114
Chapter Twenty-Two 115
How to use Apple Freeform App 115
Create a Freeform board 115

Create a new board 115
Create a board using another app 116
Open a board 117
Duplicate a board 118
Add and Format Shapes 118
Create a diagram 119
Draw or Handwrite 120
Choose Items & Scroll using Apple Pencil 121
Chapter Twenty-Three 123
How to use the Reminders App 123
Add a Reminders 123
Add a Scheduled Reminder 123
Add a Repeating Scheduled Reminder 124
Add a Location-Based Reminder 125
Chapter Twenty-Four 127
How to use Tab Groups in Safari 127
Create a Tab Group 127
Reorder Safari Tab Groups 128
Transfer a Tab to a different Tab Group ... 129
Rename a Tab Group 129
Close All Tab Group 129
Remove a Safari Tab Group 130
How to use Extensions on Safari 130
Install Safari extensions 130
Manage your Extensions 131

Use Extensions 131
Change Extension Settings 132
Delete an Extension 132
Remove Ads & Distractions in Safari 133
Show Reader 133
Enable Reader Automatically 133
Block pop-ups 134
Chapter Twenty-Five 135
How to use the Weather App 135
Check the weather 135
Enable Location Services 135
Check the Local Forecast 136
Personalize the Weather Units 136
Change the location shown in the Weather widget 137
View the weather in another Location 137
Add a Location to your weather list 138
Remove a Location in your weather list 138
Reorder Locations in your weather list 139
Enable Weather Notifications 139
Chapter Twenty-Six 141
Disable Location-Based Suggestions 141
Lock/Unlock the Screen Orientation 141
Add a Dictionary 142
View the Battery Percentage 142
Reduce Loud Headphone Sound 142

Schedule Downtime 143
Add App Limits..143
Enable Dark Mode...144
Enable True Tone 144
Add Notification Summary 145
Adjust how Notifications Appear 146
Adjust Alert Styles..146
Adjust Group Notification Settings................147
Disable Notifications for Apps 147
Adjust Notifications Appearance on Lock Screen 148
Create a Memoji 148
    Add a Memoji.. 148
    Edit a Memoji 149
Conclusion 151
About the Author..152
Index...153

Introduction

The iPad Air 2024 is also called the iPad Air 6, or the sixth-generation iPad Air. Apple revealed the tablet at its "Let Loose" event on May 7. The model introduces two distinct screen sizes for the first time: the 11-inch, weighing 462g, and the 13-inch, weighing 617g. While its predecessor, the iPad Air 2022, featured the M1 chip, Apple has upgraded the new iPad Air with the M2 chipset. You can choose from four storage options, starting with 128GB and up to 1TB. The device also boasts 8 GB of RAM. It features a liquid-retina display.

Depending on preference, users can select from the four different colors: starlight, space grey, blue, and purple.

The front camera's new positioning on the longer edge improves video calls. It features an ultra-wide camera with 12 megapixels that is landscape-oriented and is able to shoot 1080p video, whereas the rear camera is able to perform a 5x digital zoom thanks to its 12-megapixel camera. Not only that, it's able to shoot 4K video.

The Neural Engine and iPadOS enhance the iPad with AI capabilities like Live Caption and Visual Look Up, among other stunning features. In this book, you'll learn about interactive widgets, freeforms for sketching, Stage Manager, which lets users overlap multiple windows, and many more features.

Unlike the iPad Pro models, which have Face ID functionality, Apple has maintained its tradition of featuring only Touch ID on the iPad Air. The device supports 5G as well as Wi-Fi 6E connectivity. Apple has integrated a landscape stereo speaker that features spatial audio.

The iPad Air is compatible with the newly launched Apple Pencil Pro. The stylus can be charged wirelessly. Apple's addition of hover support, previously exclusive to the iPad Pro, allows users to view strokes without the need to place the Apple Pencil on the iPad's screen. Also, you can magnetically attach the Apple Pencil to the right side of the bezel when not in use.

The device supports Magic Keyboard, which transforms your iPad into a mini laptop thanks to the keyboard and trackpad.

This book aims to simplify the process of setting up and managing the various settings of your iPad Air 2024, including mastering the essential notebook features to improve your workflow and boost productivity.

Chapter One

Set up iPad

After getting your hands on your iPad, go ahead and unbox it, charge it, and then power it on to commence the setup by following the guidelines below.

- First, long-press the Power key at the upper-right corner to power on your iPad.
- Proceed by swiping upward, then choose a language.
- After that, select your region/country.
- Next up, press "**Set Up Manually**."
- For automatic sign in (for people who own an Apple device that runs on iOS 11 or more recent releases), hit "**Quick Start**" to proceed.
- Proceed by choosing your desired Wi-Fi network; input the password.
- Then choose "**Join**."
- Hit on "**Use Cellular Connection**" if you prefer to use a network provider.
- Go through the details on the "**Data & Privacy**" menu, then choose "**Continue**."
- After that, press "**Continue**" to add Touch ID.
- Input your passcode and re-enter it. For passcode alternatives, press "**Passcode

Options." Go ahead and hit on your desired option.
- Input your Apple ID and password.
- Now, choose "**Next**." If you've never registered for an Apple ID before, hit "**Create an Apple ID**." However, if you've registered before but can't remember your log in information, hit "**Forgot Password or Apple ID**."
- Next up, choose "**Agree**."
- Hit "**Continue**" to setup with the default settings or choose "**Customize Settings**" to personalize the settings.
- After that, choose "**Continue**."
- To register for Apple Pay, press "**Continue**" and go through the onscreen guide. Hit **Set Up Later in Settings**" to skip for now.
- Press "**Continue**" to setup Siri.
- Go through the onscreen prompts to configure and personalize the settings.
- Proceed by swiping up on your iPad, then choose "**Get Started**" to start using your Apple tablet.

Turn on your iPad

Long-tap the top button till the Apple symbol displays.

Set up Cellular Service

People with cellular models of the iPad can register for a cellular data plan to help them connect online when Wi-Fi is unavailable. A SIM card and subscription to a data plan by your carrier will be required regardless of whether you're using an eSIM or a physical SIM.

Set up eSIM
- Launch the Settings app.
- Next up, choose "**Cellular Data**."

- Proceed by choosing a carrier, then go through the prompts to configure your first cellular plan. Hit on "**Add a New Plan**" if you desire to include additional cellular plan.

Open Apps

You can swiftly launch an application from the home screen.

- Navigate to your iPad home screen, then swipe upward from the lower corner of the display.

- To surf through the applications, swipe either left or right.

- Click an application icon to launch it.
- To go back to the default home screen, swipe upwards from the bottom corner.

Install New iPadOS

Updating your iPad to the most recent iPadOS gives you access to new features and security enhancements. You can enable automatic or manual updates.

Install iPadOS Automatically

- Launch the Settings app.
- Then hit "**General**."
- After that, press "**Software Update**."
- Next up, press "**Automatic Updates**."
- Proceed by toggling on iOS Updates underneath "**Automatically Download**" and "**Automatically Install**"

Install iPadOS Manually

- Launch the Settings app.
- Then hit "**General**."

- Next up, choose "**Software Update**."

- Once your iPad detects an available update, press "**Download and Install**."
- After that, press "**Continue**."
- Then choose "**Install**."

Create your Apple ID

Apple ID gives you access to Apple's free and premium services including the App Store where you can download and purchase applications. If you skipped creating an Apple ID when initially setting up your iPad, then follow these guidelines.

- Launch the App Store.
- Next up, hit the My Account button.
- Tap Create New Apple ID. If you don't see this option, make sure that you're signed out of iCloud.
- Go through the prompts to input an email address, password, payment method, etc.
- Now, select "**Next**."
- Proceed by verifying your phone number and email.
- Then choose "**Next**."
- Follow the prompts to finalize.

Chapter Two

Backup your iPad

If you have your iPad backed up, you can restore the files on a different device in the event that your original iPad is damaged or gets missing.

Enable iCloud Backup

Apple iCloud offers you free storage space to back up some of your files. It can be done automatically or manually.

- Launch the Settings app.
- Proceed by tapping your name at the top.
- Next up, choose "**iCloud**."
- Then hit "**iCloud Backup**."
- Press the switch beside the "**iCloud Backup**" option to enable it.
- Then choose "**OK**." The iCloud will commence back up instantly as long as it is well charged and connected to Wi-Fi.

Manually Backup the iPad

- Launch the Settings app.
- Proceed by tapping your name at the top.
- Next up, choose "**iCloud**."

- After that, hit "**iCloud Backup**."
- Hit the toggle beside the "**iCloud Backup**" option to activate it.
- Next up, choose "**Back Up Now**."

Backup with MacBook

Mac users can have their iPad backed up on their PC running the macOS Catalina and other recent releases.

- Start by connecting your iPad to your Mac.
- Then, head to the Finder app on your Mac.
- Go ahead and select your iPad underneath "**Locations**."
- Next up, select "**Back Up Now**."
- Proceed by selecting "**Back up all of the data on your iPad to this Mac**."

Back up with Windows Computer

- Start by connecting your iPad to your PC using a cable.
- Launch the iTunes application on your PC.
- Go ahead and select the iPad icon close to the upper left of the app.
- Then select "Summary."
- Next up, hit "**Back Up Now**."

Factory Reset the iPad

When you reset your tablet, it'll remove your personal settings and restore them to default. However, your files will remain intact.

- Launch the Settings app.
- After that, choose "**General**."
- Next up, press "**Transfer or Reset iPad**."
- Go ahead and choose "**Reset**."
- Proceed by selecting "**Reset All Settings**."
- Next up, input your passcode.
- After that, hit "**Reset All Settings**" again to commence the reset.

Chapter Three

Set up Apple Pay

Apple Pay is just like Samsung Pay and Google Pay. It gives account owners leverage to shop online and make payments directly on the app or website through biometric authentication. However, to ensure seamless use of the services, you'll need to register your debit card with the Wallet application on your iPad so that you don't enter it anymore when purchasing products online or in supported physical shops.

Add a Card for Apple Pay

- Launch the Wallet app.
- Hit on the plus button at the upper-right.
- After that, choose "**Continue**" or "**Next**."
- Proceed by scanning your debit card via the onscreen camera or manually input the card's details in the input field.
- Then choose "**Next**."
- Go ahead and insert the expiration date and security code.
- Next up, choose "**Next**."
- Then select "**Agree**."
- After that, press "**Agree**" once more.

- Proceed by selecting how you wish to verify your card.
- Now, press "**Next**."
- After that, select "**Enter Code**."
- Insert the received verification code.
- Now, choose "**Next**."
- Afterward, choose "**Done**."

Adjust your Apple Pay Default Card

You can register multiple debit cards on the Wallet app, and then, when needed, you can choose your preferred one as the default card.

- Launch the Settings app.
- After that, press "**Wallet & Apple Pay**."
- Next up, hit "**Default Card**."
- Proceed by choosing the card you desired to be the default card for your transactions.

Delete your Card

You can delete any card you prefer from the Wallet app.

- Launch the Settings app.
- Afterward, hit "**Wallet & Apple Pay**."
- Go ahead and choose the card, then hit "**Remove This Card**."

Set up Apple Cash

Apple Cash is a service that lets users send and receive funds. The users can use these funds to purchase in-app items or at a physical store.

- Launch the Settings app.
- Move down and hit on "**Wallet & Apple Pay**."
- Proceed by turning on "**Apple Cash**."
- Then hit on "**Apple Cash**" underneath "**Payment Cards**."
- Next up, hit "**Continue**."
- Go through the prompts to finalize the setup.

Add Money to Apple Cash Card

You'll need to fund your Apple Cash card before attempting to send money.

- Launch the Wallet app.
- Go ahead and select your Apple Cash card.
- Then hit on the triple dots at the upper-right.

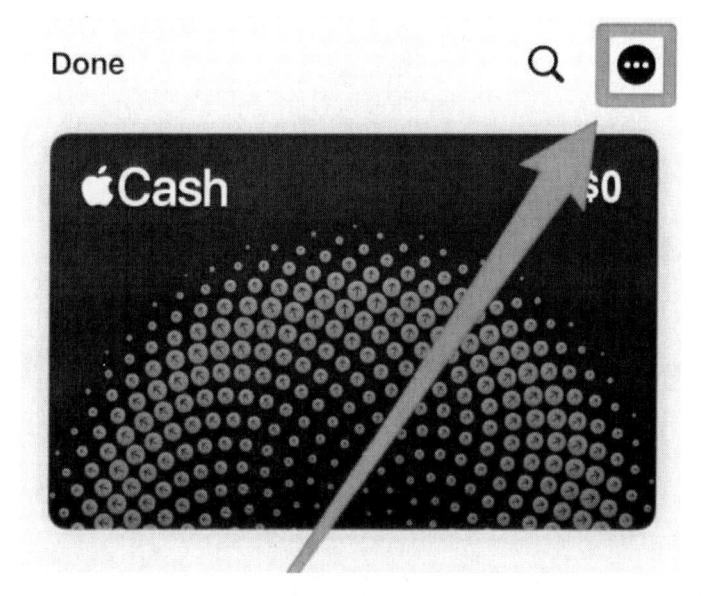

- After that, hit "**Add Money**."

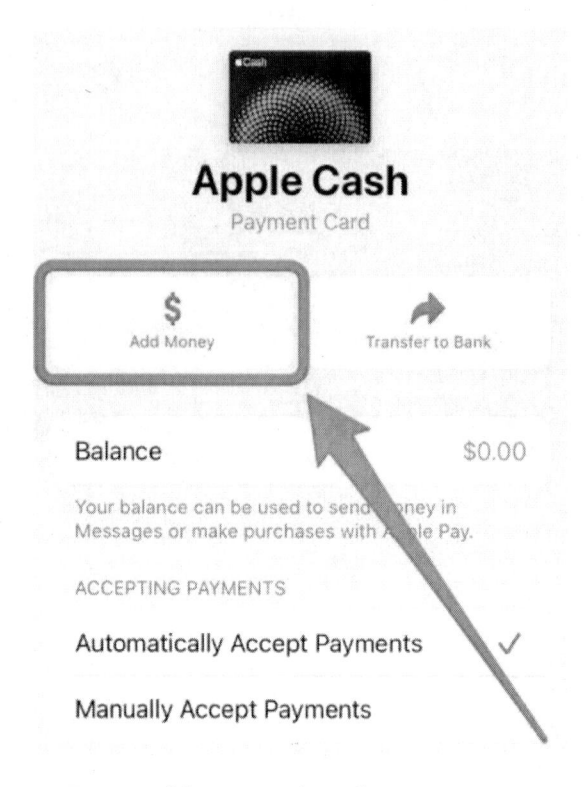

- Proceed by entering the amount.
- Lastly, choose "**Add**."

Send & Receive Funds

After funding your Apple Cash card, you can then send funds to your loved ones. Also, you can request that your debtors pay you through Apple Cash too.

Ensure the receiver or person you're requesting money from has an Apple device.

- Launch the iMessage app.

- Navigate to a conversation you had with the contact you wish to send or request money from.
- Then, select the App store button beside the iMessage text box.
- After that, select the **Apple Pay** button.

- Proceed by inputting an amount.
- Next up, select "**Pay**" or "**Request**."

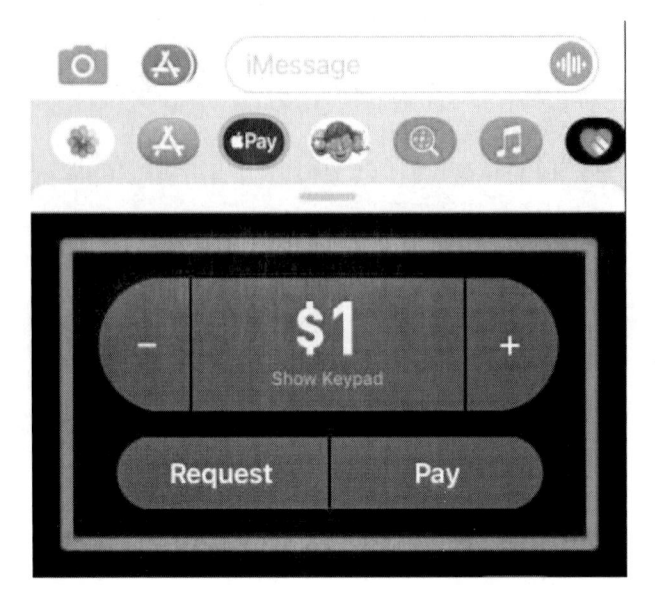

- To send money, press the Send button and authenticate the transaction with Touch ID or password. If you're requesting to be paid, the contact will have to confirm it first.

Verify your Apple Pay Identity

You should be prompted to confirm your Apple Pay identity during the initialization process, if not, then follow the guideline.

- Launch the Settings app.
- Then, select "**Wallet & Apple Pay**."
- Next up, hit "**Apple Pay Cash**."
- After this, choose "**Verify Identity**."
- Now, hit "**Continue**."
- Proceed by inputting your names, then choose "**Next**."

- Go ahead and insert your address.
- Then choose "**Next**."
- Fill in the last four digits of your social security number and your date of birth.
- Then choose "**Next**."
- Go through the prompts to finalize the setup.

Chapter Four

Set up Family Sharing

By setting up Family Sharing, you'll be able to add five people that share access to Apple services, iCloud subscription, purchases, etc.

Set up a Family Sharing Group
- Launch the Settings app.
- Proceed by tapping your name at the upper menu.
- Then choose "**Family**."
- Go through the prompts to set up and add people.

Add a Family Member
The Family member you intend to add should have an Apple ID

- Launch the Settings app.
- Next, select "**Family**."
- After that, select .
- Then choose "**Invite Others**."
- Follow the prompts.

Set up an Apple ID for your Kid

- Launch the Settings app.
- Next, select "**Family**."
- Then select .
- Next up, choose "**Create Child Account**."
- Follow the prompts.

Delete a Member

When you remove someone from the group, the shared content will become inaccessible and their access revoked.

- Launch the Settings app.
- Next, select "**Family**."
- Proceed by selecting the person's name.
- Next up, hit "**Remove [person's name] from Family**."

Exit a Family Sharing Group

Once you exit the group, you'll not be able to share your contents and purchases with members, and you'll be unable to access their shared content.

If the group was set up by you, then the group will be disbanded after you leave.

- Launch the Settings app.

- Next, select "**Family**."
- Then choose your name.
- After that, hit "**Stop Using Family Sharing**."

Chapter Five

How to use Touch ID

The iPad Air only supports Touch ID unlike the Pro models that offers facial authentication.

Add Touch ID
- Launch the Settings app.
- After that, hit "**Touch ID & Passcode.**"

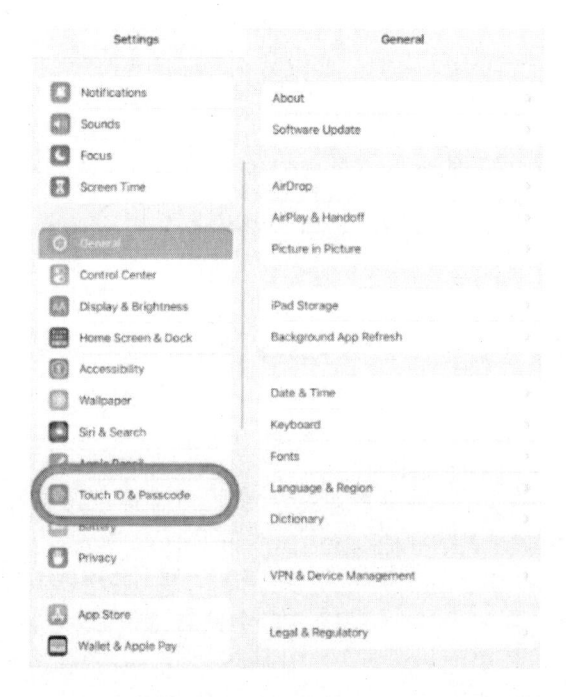

- Proceed by inputting your preferred six-number passcode.
- Next up, hit "**Add a Fingerprint**."

- Go through the prompts to finish up.

Add Fingerprints Name

You can register several fingers on the Touch ID and name each with a different name for easy identification.

- Launch the Settings app.
- Next up, hit "**Touch ID & Passcode**."
- Go ahead and press the fingerprint's name underneath the "**Fingerprints**" section.
- Proceed by inputting a new name.
- Then choose "**Done**."

Remove a Fingerprint

- Launch the Settings app.
- Next up, hit "**Touch ID & Passcode**."
- Proceed by resting your registered finger on the tablet's top button.
- Then select the fingerprint.
- Lastly, choose "**Delete Fingerprint**."

Disable Touch ID

You can disable Touch ID if you no longer need it.

- Launch the Settings app.
- Next up, hit "**Touch ID & Passcode**."
- Proceed by turning off Touch ID.

Unlock the iPad with Touch ID

- Start by placing your registered finger on the top button.

- If you need to lock your iPad once more, tap the top button.

Set a Passcode

By adding a passcode, users can increase the security of their iPad by entering the code before their iPad wakes or turns on.

Set the Passcode
- Launch the Settings app.
- Next up, hit "**Touch ID & Passcode**."
- After that, choose "**Turn Passcode On**."
- For additional options, choose "**Passcode Options**."

Adjust Automatic Lock
- Launch the Settings app.
- After that, hit "**Display & Brightness**."
- Then select "**Auto-Lock**."

- Proceed by setting a time duration.

Delete Data after 10 Failed Passcodes

You can configure your iPad to wipe all data, including photos, videos, and settings, after 10 unsuccessful tries at entering the passcode.

- Launch the Settings app.
- After that, hit "**Touch ID & Passcode**."
- Proceed by toggling on "**Erase Data**."

Disable the Passcode
- Launch the Settings app.

- After that, hit **"Touch ID & Passcode."**
- Then hit on **"Turn Passcode Off."**

Chapter Six

Add your Mail, Calendars & Contacts

The iPad just like other smartphones offers you the option to either import your email, contacts and calendar or set up a fresh account.

Add Google Account
- Launch the Settings app.
- Then hit "**Mail**."
- After that, select "**Accounts**."
- Next up, choose "**Add Account**."
- Then press "**Google**."
- Now hit "**Continue**."
- Proceed by inputting your Google account details.
- Then press the toggle beside the Mails, Contacts, and Calendars options to enable them.
- Afterward, choose "**Save**."

Add Outlook.com Account
- Launch the Settings app.
- Next up, choose "**Mail**."
- Hit on "**Accounts**."
- After that, hit "**Add Account**."

- Then select "**Outlook.com**."
- Go ahead and input your Outlook.com account details.
- Then press the toggle beside the Mails, Contacts, and Calendars options to enable them.
- Afterward, choose "**Save**."

Add Exchange Mail Account

- Head to the Settings app.
- Then choose "**Mail**."
- Next up, select "**Accounts**."
- Now, choose "**Add Account**."
- Afterward, select "**Exchange**."
- Proceed by inputting your Exchange email address.
- Now, select "**Next**."
- Next up, press "**Configure Manually**."
- Proceed by insetring your Exchange account details to manually register the account.
- After that, choose "**Next**."
- Then hit the toggle beside the Mails, Contacts, and Calendars options to turn them on.
- Then, press "**Save**."

Add Default Email Account

Assuming you have multiple emails registered on your iPad, you can set one of them as the default.

- Launch the Settings app.
- Now, select "**Mail**."
- Next up, choose "**Default Account**."
- Go ahead and hit your preferred default account.

Remove Email Account

- Launch the Settings app.
- Afterward, hit "**Mail**."
- Then select "**Accounts**."
- Proceed by selecting your preferred email account.
- Afterward, choose "**Delete Account**."
- Next up, press "**Delete from My iPad**."

How to use Hide My Email

Hide My Email is an exclusive service for people with an iCloud+ subscription. The service lets users mask their primary email address while using a proxy or secondary email address to sign up on websites.

The website only stores the proxy email address, and the user's real email address is never revealed, but the messages that are delivered to the proxy address are sent to the user's primary email address. To use this, the user must first generate a Hide My Email address.

Add Hide My Email Address

- Launch the Settings app.
- Then select your name from the top of the Settings window.
- Next up, choose "**iCloud**."
- After that, hit "**Hide My Email**."
- From there, select "**Create new address**."
- Then choose "**Continue**."
- Proceed by inserting a label for the address to help you recall the reason for creating it.
- Once the email address has been generated, choose "**Done**."

View Apps that use Hide My Email Address

You can see the applications that uses the Hide My Email.

- Launch the Settings app.

- Go ahead and press your name from the top of the Settings window.
- Next up, choose "**iCloud**."
- After that, hit "**Hide My Email**." You can then see the various applications and platforms that uses "**Hide My Email Address**." Choose an option to unveil the email address.

Disable Forwarding for a Hide My Email Address

You can ensure that messages that you receive at the generated email address are not sent to your real email address.

- Launch the Settings app.
- Proceed by tapping your name from the top of the Settings window.
- Then select "**iCloud**."
- Hit on "**Hide My Email**."
- Choose the app/website you wish to unsubscribe from receiving emails.
- Proceed by hitting the toggle beside the "**Forward to**" option to disable it.
- Then choose "**Turn off**."

Personalize the Hide My Email Forwarding Address

You can adjust the email address that receive the messages sent to the generated proxy email.

- Launch the Settings app.
- Choose your name from the top of the Settings window.
- Next up, hit "**iCloud**."
- From there, choose "**Hide My Email**."
- Then choose "**Forward to**."
- Go ahead and pick the email address that the emails will be sent.

Chapter Seven

Connect Apple Pencil to iPad

Apple Pencil let users doodle, write, sketch and colour their artwork, among other functions.

Pair the Apple Pencil

To use the Apple Pencil, you'll have to pair it with your iPad. Ensure that Bluetooth is enabled on your iPad before you begin.

- Start by taking out the cover of your Apple Pencil, then plug the Pencil with its USB-C cord into the adapter.
- Proceed by plugging the other end into your iPad.
- When prompted, select "**Pair**" to link the two gadgets. Once the connection is established, detach from the adapter and begin to use the Apple Pencil on your iPad.

Disconnect the Apple Pencil

You can unlink the Apple Pencil from your iPad, if needed.

- Launch the Settings app.

- Then choose "**Bluetooth**."
- Go ahead and select your Apple Pencil from the list of displayed Bluetooth devices.
- Next up, choose the "**i**" icon beside the Apple Pencil.
- Then press "**Forget this Device**."

View the Apple Pencil Battery

In order to access the battery level of the Apple Pencil, you'll need to install a widget.

- Long-tap a widget or a blank area on your iPad home screen till it jiggles.
- Then select the plus button.
- Go ahead and hit the battery level widget.
- Afterward, select "**Add Widget**."
- Next up, choose "**Done**."
- Proceed by swiping left to access Today View. From there, you can view your Apple Pencil battery level.

Charge the Apple Pencil

- For Apple Pencil (2nd-generation), start by attaching your Apple Pencil to the magnetic connector positioned on the longer side of the tablet.
- Once connected, you should see the battery level displayed at the upper section of the screen.

- If you're using the USB-C type, then pull the end of the Apple Pencil, then plug in the USB-C charging cord. Go ahead and attach the other end of the cord to your iPad.

Chapter Eight

How to use AirDrop

AirDrop enables the nearby wireless transfer of images, files, movies, etc., to compatible Apple devices and Macs.

Before starting out, your Bluetooth and Wi-Fi are enabled. Also, ensure that the recipient have their AirDrop settings to "Everyone" or "Contacts Only."

Send an Item
- Head to the content you intend to transfer.
- Hit the Share or the three dots icon to see the sharing options.

- Next up, choose "**AirDrop**".
- Proceed by selecting your preferred recipient.

Enable others to send Files to your iPad
- Visit the Control Center.
- Long-tap the upper-left set of controls.
- Hit .

- Then hit "**Contacts Only**" or another option to select who'll be sending items via AirDrop to you.

Disable Cellular Data for AirDrop

You may be charged for cellular data whenever you use AirDrop. You can

If can restrict cellular data usage whenever Bluetooth or Wi-Fi are unavailable.

- Launch the Settings app.
- Next up, hit "**General**."
- Then, select "**AirDrop**."
- Proceed by disable the "**Use Cellular Data**" toggle.

Change AirDrop settings

You can select if your contacts alone will see your iPad and transfer items to you via AirDrop or if everyone with a supported device can do it.

- Launch the Settings app.
- Next up, hit "**General**."
- Go ahead and press "**AirDrop**."
- Select an option.

Accept AirDrop

If someone is sending an item via AirDrop to you, you'll receive a notification. Select "**Accept**" to receive it or "**Decline**" to ignore.

Chapter Nine

How to use the Control Center

Opening the Control Center gives you quick access and shortcuts to frequently used features such as Wi-Fi, camera, Bluetooth, and more.

Open the Control Center

To launch the Control Center, drag down your finger from the upper right corner of your iPad screen where you have the battery icon.

Touch and hold to see Camera options.

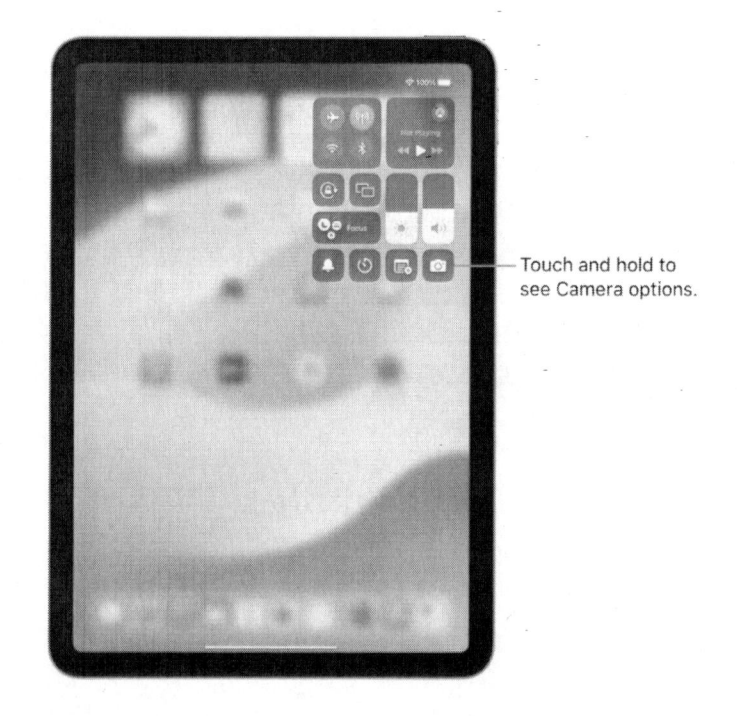

Customize the Control Center

You can select the buttons and icons that are displayed in the Control Center.

- Launch the Settings app.
- Then select "**Control Center**."
- To add icons to the Control Center, press the plus button next to the application or shortcut.
- To disable the shortcut from the Control Center, press the red minus button, then hit "**Remove**."

Organize the Control Center

You can reorder or reposition a shortcut in the Control Center.

- Launch the Settings app.
- Next up, select "**Control Center**."
- Proceed by hitting the three horizontal lines next to a shortcut, then drag it upward or downward.

Temporarily Disable a Wi-Fi

- Navigate to the Control Center.
- From there, hit 📶 .
- To reconnect, hit it once more.
- If you need to view the connected Wi-Fi name, long-tap 📶 .

Temporarily Disable Bluetooth

- Navigate to the Control Center.
- From there, hit 🔵 . Click it once more to authorize connection.

Disable Access to Control Center in Apps

- Launch the Settings app.
- Next up, hit "**Control Center**."
- Proceed by disable the "**Access Within Apps**" option.

Open Additional Controls in Control Center

Some controls show more options when you long-tap on them.

- Long-tap the upper-left set of controls, then hit 🛜.
- Long-tap 📷 to capture image, video, etc.

Chapter Ten

How to use Quick Note

Quick Note offers you a quick access to write down ideas, save URLS, and other tasks you'd normally do in the Notes app.

Open Quick Note

You can swiftly head to the Quick Note menu regardless of your current screen.

- Start by dragging your fingers upward from the bottom-right corner of your iPad. Next up, the Quick Note menu will appear.

- Go ahead and press any icon or button on the Quick Note menu to write, insert or import items.
- To view the Quick Note from the Notes app, press the grid button.

Add Links to Quick Note

If you intend to insert a link on your Quick Note, it can be done using two methods.

Create a Link when you Create a Quick Note

- Head to the Safari browser and open the webpage where you wish to copy the URL.
- Quickly open the Quick Note menu by swiping your fingers upward from the bottom-right corner.
- Press the compose button.

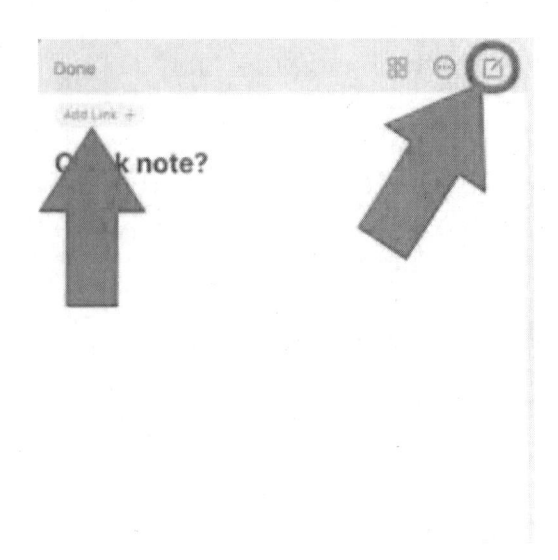

- From there, press "**Add Link**." The copied link will be added to your Quick Note.

Create a Link via Text in Quick Note
- Launch Safari and head to the web address you desire to copy the content.
- Proceed by swiping your fingers upward from the bottom-right corner to launch the Quick Notes menu.
- Then long-press and move the selector tool to select the text that you intend to copy.
- Afterward, press "**Add to Quick Note**."

Delete a Quick Note
- Head to the Quick Note menu.
- Then press the three dots button.
- After that, choose "**Delete**."

Share a Quick Note
- Head to the Quick Note menu.
- Then press the three dots button.
- Next, select "**Share**."
- Proceed by choosing the contacts you desire to send the Quick Note.

Print a Quick Note
- Head to the Quick Note menu.
- Then press the three dots button.
- Next, select "**Share**."
- After that, choose "**Print**."
- Hit on the "**Printer**" submenu to select a printer.
- Then press "**Print**."

Chapter Eleven

How to use Stage Manager

Stage Manager let you multitask. with it, users can overlap multiple windows, adjust window size, click to alternate between applications, etc.

You can even group applications for particular tasks, overlay, reposition and set up to your liking. If you connect the iPad to an external monitor, you can even move windows between the external monitor and your iPad thanks to Stage Manager.

Enable Stage Manager

To multitask using Stage Manager, you'll have to turn on the multitasking feature. There are two ways to do that:

Method one:

- Start by swiping down from the top right corner to launch the Control Center.
- Then select the Stage Manager button to activate it.

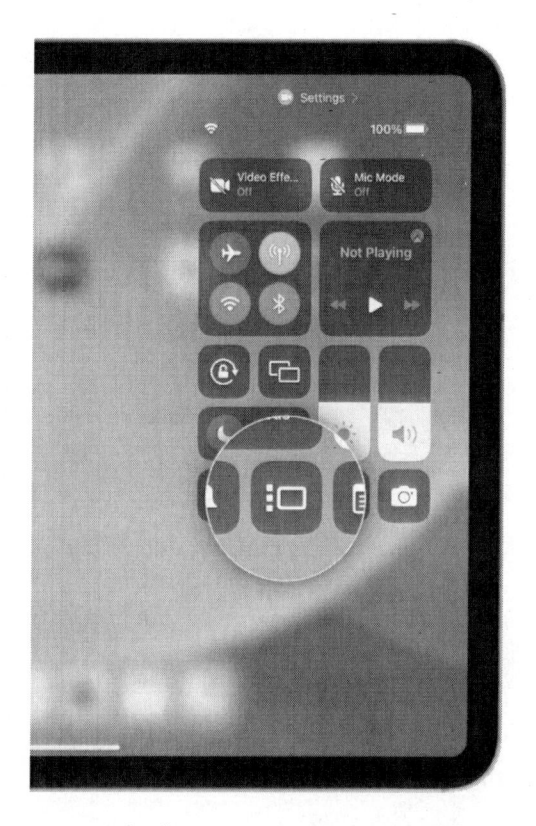

- Press the button again to disable it.

Method two:

- Launch the Settings app.
- Then hit on "**Multitasking & Gestures**."
- From there, choose "**Stage Manager**."

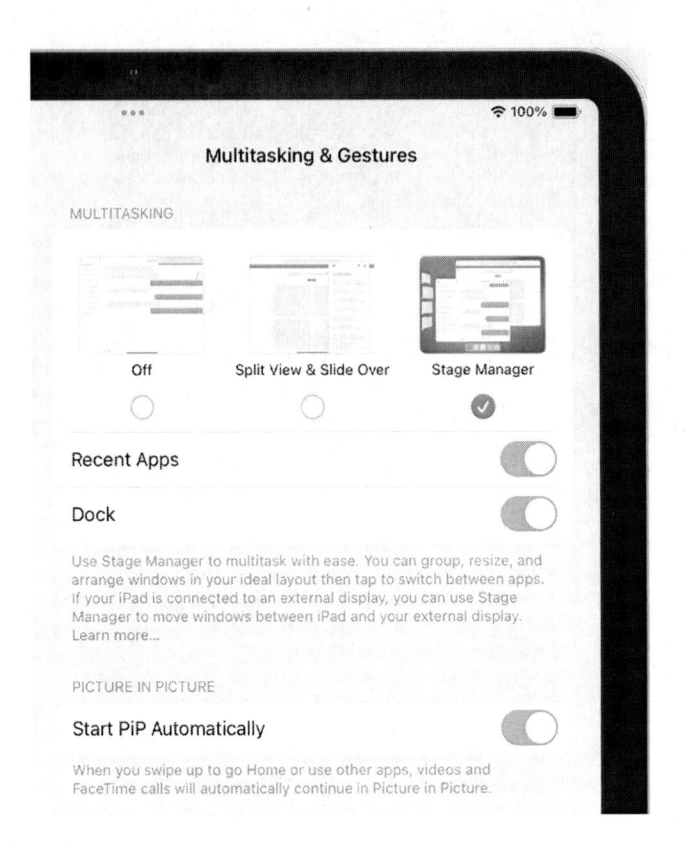

Multitasking with Multiple Windows

If there's an application you're currently using and wish to navigate to another app and group them together, then do this:

- Hit ![icon] from the top of the menu.
- Next up, select "**Add Another Window**." Your currently active

windows will slide away to display the recent application windows. Just click on one to add it.

- Long-tap an application from the Recent applications menu, then proceed by dragging it to the current window at the middle of the display.
- Long-press an application from the Dock, then proceed by dragging it upward to the middle of the display.
- Click the App Library button (it is the rightmost symbol in the Dock), long-tap an application icon under the App Library, proceed by dragging it from there to the middle of the display.
- When using multiple applications, you can perform these actions:
- Scale a window: Drag from the edge indented with a dark curve. However, if you're using a trackpad/mouse, simply drag from any corner of the interface.
- Relocate a menu to the Recent apps list: Hit ● ● ● on the top of the interface, then press "**Minimize**."
- Reposition a window: With your finger on the screen, pull from the upper section of the window.
- Make a window larger: Hit ● ● ● from the top of the interface, then press "**Enter Full Screen**."

Switch between Apps

A simple switching of applications can b done by clicking another application from the Recent apps, or select an icon from the Dock

The app you're currently using will occupy the center of your iPad screen. If you tapped the "Recent Apps," they'll display on the left side, whereas the Dock will still appear at the bottom.

There are other methods to switch applications:

- Swipe upward from the lower section of the display, then hold on in the middle of the display to view the recent applications and groups.
- Swipe horizontally along the bottom corner of the display.
- Swipe horizontally using four/five fingers.

Hide/Show the Recent Apps List

Method one:

- Navigate to the Control Center.

- Long-tap the Stage Manager icon

- Proceed by tapping the checkmark beside the image.

Method two:

- Launch the Settings app.
- Next up, hit "**Multitasking & Gestures**."
- Go ahead and tick the "**Stage Manager**" checkbox to enable it, then enable or disable "**Recent Apps**."

Close a Window

- Hit on .
- Then select "**Close**."
- The window will go away from the grouping if it's part of a group of applications.

Transfer an App to an External Monitor

By connecting your tablet to an external monitor, you can perform tasks across the two screens by simply dragging applications and windows between the screens and organize them to your desired layout.

You can navigate applications between displays through either of these:

- Drag from the upper section of the application window to position it from one screen to another.

- Drag the application icon you intend to move.

How to use Picture in Picture

Picture in Picture enables you to view and use two screens or applications simultaneously. With this, you can surf the internet and watch movies at once.

When you're watching a movie, select .

The movie interface will shrink to the edge of the display; this will let you view your home screen and launch other applications. While your video interface is showing, you can perform some actions:

Adjust the video interface: To enlarge the video interface, pinch wide. Pinch close to reduce its size.

View & hide controls: Click the video interface.

Reposition the video interface: To move the window, start by dragging it to your preferred corner on the display.

Hide the video interface: Start by dragging it off the right or left corner of the display.

Exit the video interface: Hit the Close icon .

Go back to a full video display: Hit on the picture icon  in the small video interface.

Chapter Twelve

How to use Slide Over window

You can make an application float in front of another application or window, and you can then switch between the app in front and the one behind, thanks to Slide Over. For instance, if you're going through the Photos app, you can have a messaging app appear in the Slide Over window and respond to your messages while still viewing your pictures in the Photos app.

Open an App in Slide Over
- When you're on an application, hit ● ● ● on the upper screen, then choose ▢.
- The application you are currently on will slide to the side to allow the Home Screen and Dock appear.
- Navigate to and select the application you intend to display at the back of the Slide Over interface.
- Once the second application opens, the first application will now pop up in a Slide Over interface just in front of it.

Switch between Apps

Swiping right around the bottom of the Slide Over menu will let you switch between applications. There's another way:

- Start by swiping midway upward on the display from the lower part of the Slide Over pane, halt, then raise your finger.
- The whole Slide Over pane will display.
- Go ahead and choose the application you intend to view, if it appears visible. Swipe horizontally across the applications if it doesn't appear.

Move the Slide Over window

- To position the Slide Over pane to the opposite of the screen: just drag from the three dots icon ● ● ● at the upper menu of the Slide Over pane.
- Temporarily remove the Slide Over pane: Staring from the lower section of the Slide Over pane, swipe upward, swipe the ● ● ●.
- You can make the Slide Over pane return to the screen by dragging the tab that represents the Slide Over pane from the left corner of the display.

Change Slide Over to Split View

- From the upper menu of the Slide Over pane, select the three dots icon ● ● ●.
- Then hit ▢▢ .
- Next up, choose ▮▯ to make the application you're currently on display on the left. Or select ▯▮ to have it on the right.

Open a File in the Middle of the Screen

Some applications let you open a task in the middle of the application window.

- For the Mail app, long-tap a message in your mailbox. For Messages, long-tap a conversation. For Notes: Long-tap a note.
- Then hit "**Open in New Window**."
- You should see the task open up in the middle of the display.
- To adjust the middle window to full screen, hit ▢ . To make it appear in

Split View window, hit ▢. For Slide Over window, hit ▢.

How to use Split View

The iPad offers the advantage of working with multiple applications simultaneously. You can launch two separate applications, or two windows of the same application, dividing the screen into adjustable views.

Open a Second App in Split View

- When you're on an application, hit ● ● ● from the upper menu.
- Next, select ▢.
- Next up, choose ▢ to make the application you're currently on display on the left. Or select ▢ to have it on the right.
- The current app will roll over to the side to display the Home Screen and Dock.

- From the Dock or Home screen, go ahead and choose the second application. The first and second apps will then display in Split View.

Replace an App

If two applications appear in Split View, you can substitute either of them with another applications.

- Swipe downward from the three dots ● ● ● at the upper menu of the application you intend to substitute.
- The application you prefer to substitute will slide down, while the other application will slide to the side to show the Home Screen and Dock.
- Proceed by selecting the application replacement from the Home Screen or Dock by tapping tap it.
- You should now see both applications pop up in Split View.

Chapter Thirteen

How to use Universal Control

Universal Control enables users to seamlessly connect their iPad to their Mac and move between both devices with a mouse or trackpad.

To ensure a seamless connection, the iPad and Mac should be running on the same iCloud account with the 2FA turned on. Also, Wi-Fi and Bluetooth must be enabled.

Furthermore, the distance between both devices ought not to exceed 10 meters.

Enable Universal Control on Mac

- Turn on your Mac, then select the Apple icon in the upper left.
- Next up, choose "**System Preferences**."
- From there, hit "**Displays**."
- Then select "**Universal Control**."
- Proceed by ticking the options that displays on the screen. For newer macOS, choose the Advanced button.
- After that, choose "**Done**."

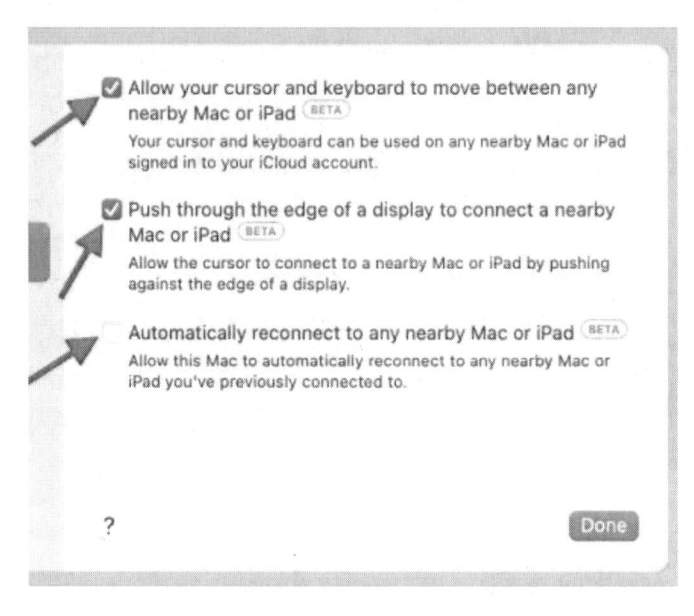

> ☑ Allow your cursor and keyboard to move between any nearby Mac or iPad (BETA)
> Your cursor and keyboard can be used on any nearby Mac or iPad signed in to your iCloud account.
>
> ☑ Push through the edge of a display to connect a nearby Mac or iPad (BETA)
> Allow the cursor to connect to a nearby Mac or iPad by pushing against the edge of a display.
>
> ☐ Automatically reconnect to any nearby Mac or iPad (BETA)
> Allow this Mac to automatically reconnect to any nearby Mac or iPad you've previously connected to.
>
> ?   Done

- Then choose "**Add Display**."
- Go ahead and choose the Mac that shows up underneath the "**Link Keyboard & Mouse**" header.

Enable Universal Control on iPad

- Launch the Settings app.
- Then hit on "**General**."
- From there, hit "**AirPlay & Handoff**."
- Next up, press "**Cursor and Keyboard**."
- Proceed by dragging the trackpad or mouse to the corner of the iPad or Mac to manage the screen.

Connect your Devices

- Bring the Mac and iPad closer to each other.
- Proceed by using a trackpad or mouse to drag the indicator over the right or left corner of the display toward the path of the iPad or MacBook.
- Once you start dragging the pointer across the corner of the display, the other device will display the pointer starting to appear on screen. To switch to the device, drag the pointer in that direction.

How to use iPad as Second Monitor

To boost your workflow, you can utilize your iPad as a second monitor, mirroring the display of your Mac.

- Start by clicking the Control Center icon in the menu bar of the Mac.

- After that, select "**Display**."
- Go ahead and hit your iPad that displays underneath the "**Connect To**" header.
- Then choose to display the Sidebar on the right or left.
- From there, select the Touch Bar to show up at the bottom or top.
- Next up, toggle on "**Enable double-tap with the Apple Pencil.**"

Chapter Fourteen

How to use Siri

Thanks to Siri, by pressing the Home button on the iPad, users can get answers to any question, such as "Is it going to rain today?" or enable features (such as Bluetooth, Focus mode, etc.) on their iPad using a voice command.

Enable Siri
- Launch the Settings app.
- Then hit on "**Siri & Search**."
- Proceed by hitting the toggle beside the "**Press Home for Siri**" option.
- Then select "**Enable Siri**."

Disable Siri
- Navigate to the "**Siri & Search**" menu.
- Then hit the toggle next to "**Listen for "Hey Siri**."
- Press the beside the "**Press Home for Siri**" option.
- Choose "**Continue**."
- Then follow the prompts.

After Siri is enabled, users can start using it to get answers to questions and enable features on their tablet, start by pressing the Home button on the iPad, then say the command.

Change Siri's Language
- Launch the Settings app.
- Next up, hit "**Siri & Search**."
- After this, choose "**Language**."
- Proceed by selecting your preferred language.

Change Siri's Voice
- Launch the Settings app.
- After that, hit "**Siri & Search**."
- Then select "**Siri Voice**."
- Go ahead and select a different voice or variety.

Chapter Fifteen

How to use Widgets

Widgets are a great feature that display updates and essential information at a glance. You can even use them to arrange your home screen and Today View to your liking.

Add Widget to Home Screen

- Start by locating an empty space on the Home screen where you prefer to position the widget, then press firmly on that area.
- Go ahead and press the plus icon on the lower-left corner.
- Then select the application that you desire to add its widget.
- Proceed by swiping right or left to see the available styles.
- Then choose "**Add Widget**."
- The widget should now display on the Home Screen. Simply, drag and drop them anywhere on the screen to reorder them if you wish.
- After that, choose "**Done**."

Add Widgets in Today View

When you continuously swipe right on your iPad, you'll hit the last screen where you can't swipe any further; that's the "Today View" menu.

- Swipe to the Today View menu.
- Long-tap on the empty space of the Today View menu.
- Then choose the plus icon on the upper left corner.
- Proceed by selecting or searching for a widget.
- Go ahead and swipe left/right to choose your preferred widget size.
- After that, select "**Add Widget**."
- Once the widget appears, choose "**Done**" to save it.

Remove Widgets from Today's View

- Long-tap on a widget.
- Next up, select "**Remove Widget**."
- Then hit "**Remove**."

Stack Widgets

The iPad let users organize widgets of the same size to occupy more screen space thanks to stacking.

- Start by long-tapping the widget you prefer to add to the stack.

- Proceed by dragging and dropping the widget on top of a different widget of the same size to create a stack.

Personalize a Stack Widget
- Long-press on the widget stack.
- Then choose "**Edit Stack**."
- To rearrange, drag the widgets to the top or bottom to.
- To remove, press the minus button, then hit "**Remove**."
- Next up, choose "**Done**."

Personalize your Widgets
- Long-press on the widget.
- Then select "**Edit Widget**."
- Proceed by selecting the widget you prefer to edit.

Chapter Sixteen

How to Reorder Apps

You can make the iPad home screen look the way you want by creating folders, adding apps, removing apps, adding pages, and so much more.

Enable Edit Mode

Pressing hard on an app icon will bring up certain options, which you can tap to customize the home screen.

- Start by long-tapping on an application icon that you desire to move.
- From the popover option, hit "**Edit Home Screen**."
- Choose an option from the context menu that appears.

Reorder Apps

- Press hard on the application you intend to move.
- Drag the app to a new position once it starts to jiggle.
- Hit somewhere on the home screen to exit the jiggle mode.

Move Apps across Pages

You can move an application from one page to another so that you can conveniently see it on the home screen or swipe to see it on another page.

- Press hard on the application that you wish to move onto another page.
- Drag the application or use your other finger to swipe to the page where you intend to keep the application.
- Then let go of your finger to keep the application on the desired page.
- Touch anywhere on the screen to close the edit mode.

Remove Apps from Home Screen

Let's say you intend to delete an application from the home or app screen, what do you do?

App Screen:

- Long-tap an application to make it jiggle.
- Then hit the "**Delete App.**"
- Now hit "**Delete.**"

Home screen:

- Long-tap an application to make it jiggle.
- Next, click "**Remove App.**"

- Now hit "**Delete App**."
- If you want it to remain in the App Library, hit on "**Remove from the Home Screen....**"

Create a Home Screen Folder for Apps

Folders allow you to properly manage the applications on the home screen. Adding apps to a folder can bring about an organization on the home screen.

- Long-tap on an application on the home screen.
- Now select "**Edit Home Screen**."
- Once the application starts jiggling, drag it onto a different application to generate a folder.
- Touch anywhere outside the folder to exit it.

Rename Home Screen Folders

- Press hard on the folder, then hit "**Rename**."
- Input a new folder name.
- Hit "**Done**."
- Touch outside the folder twice to exit the page.

Transfer App from Folder to the Home Screen

Moving an application from a folder to the home screen can make it easier to locate that app.

- Navigate to the home screen, where you have the folder from which you want to drag out the application.
- Hit on the folder to see its content.
- Press hard on the desired application to make it jiggle.
- Proceed by dragging the application from the folder onto the home screen.

Delete a Folder

Dragging out all the applications on a folder will automatically delete the folder.

- Click on a folder to see its content.
- Proceed by dragging all the applications out of the folder.

Reset the Home Screen & Apps

When you reset the home screen, it will return to the way it was originally made before you started customizing it.

- Navigate to Settings.
- Hit "**General**."
- Now select "**Reset**."
- After this, hit on "**Reset Home Screen Layout**."

Chapter Seventeen

How to use FaceTime

With the FaceTime application, users can video call their family and friends from any location. It also has an audio call feature that lets you keep in touch remotely.

Make FaceTime Call
- Launch the FaceTime app.
- Next up, press "**New FaceTime**."
- Go ahead and input the contact's number you wish to dial.
- Next up, select 🎥 or 📞 icon to start the call.

Create a FaceTime Call Link
You can generate a FaceTime link that will be sent to the recipients to join the FaceTime call. Even Android and Windows users can join the call through the URL.

- Launch the FaceTime app.
- Next up, hit "**Create Link**."
- Then select "**Add Name**" to name the link you wish to generate.
- Then choose "**OK**."

- Proceed by selecting how to share the link with the intended participants.
- After sending the link, the recipients will have to tap it, and then you'll approve their request to join.

Delete a FaceTime Call Link

When you delete a FaceTime link, you're revoking access to the FaceTime session, so people will be unable to join.

- Launch the FaceTime app.
- Proceed by swiping left on the FaceTime link.
- Next up, choose "**Delete**."
- Then choose "**Delete Link**."

Use SharePlay in FaceTime

You can share your screen during FaceTime, enabling the FaceTime participants to view what's currently playing or streaming on your iPad thanks to the SharePlay feature. For example, you can show them a PowerPoint presentation or play a video.

Turn on SharePlay

To start using SharePlay, you'll have to enable it in the Settings app.

- Launch the Settings app.

- Next up, hit "**FaceTime**."
- After that, select "**SharePlay**." Proceed by tapping the toggle to enable it.

Use SharePlay to Play Music

Once you've turned on SharePlay, you can then use it to share the music or video you're currently playing on your iPad.

- Launch the FaceTime app.
- Then select "**Create Link**" to generate a FaceTime URL that will be sent to the participants.
- Once they've joined the FaceTime session, swipe upward to see your home screen.
- Navigate to the Apple Music application.
- Proceed by selecting the music you prefer to share with the participants. The SharePlay button will appear on the screen, click it.

- If the FaceTime participants' devices have active subscriptions to the service you're playing from, the music will start playing. If they don't have an existing subscription, they'll be prompted to register.

Use SharePlay to Stream Videos
- Launch the FaceTime app.
- Next up, hit "**Create Link**" to generate a FaceTime URL that will be forwarded to the participants.
- After they've joined the FaceTime session, swipe upward to view your home screen.
- Navigate to the Apple TV app.
- Go ahead and select the video you desire to watch, then select the Play button.

Turn on Portrait Mode for FaceTime

Thanks to the Portrait feature, you can avoid people seeing what your room or location looks like during a FaceTime call by blurring your background.

- Launch the FaceTime app.
- Proceed by swiping down from the upper right corner to access the Control Center.
- Then choose "**Video Effects**."

- After that, hit "**Portrait**."

Turn on Voice Isolation

During a FaceTime call, you can enable Voice Isolation to block the ambient noise so that the participants can only hear your voice.

- Start by swiping downward from the upper right corner of your iPad to access the Control Center during a FaceTime session.
- Next up, hit "**Mic Mode**."
- After that, press "**Voice Isolation**" to restrict the ambient noise.

Turn on Wide Spectrum

On the other hand, you can activate Wide Spectrum so that they can hear you as well as the background noise.

- Swipe downward from the upper right corner of your iPad to access the Control Center during a FaceTime session.
- After that, choose "**Mic Mode**."
- Then hit on "**Wide Spectrum**" to allow the background noises.

Enable Center Stage

Thanks to Center Stage, you can see everyone during a FaceTime video call, even if they're in motion.

- Launch the FaceTime app.
- Swipe downward from the upper right corner to show the Control Center .
- Then select the "**Video Effects**" button.
- After that, hit on "**Centre Stage**" to enable it.

Chapter Eighteen

How to use Focus Mode

Focus mode enables users to control which notifications they wish to receive and restrict them at a particular time and even at a specific location. You can even set exemptions for the contacts that can call you and who can't call you when the focus mode is enabled.

Enable a Focus Mode
- Launch the Settings app.
- Next up, select "**Focus**."
- Proceed by selecting from the listed focus mode; Personal, Driving, Work, etc.

- Go ahead and select "**People**" to customize the people you want to accept or decline their calls/messages during focus mode. Choose "**Allow Notifications**" to allow or "**Silence Notifications**" to mute notifications from the selected contacts. Then choose the plus button and choose the contacts.
- Select "**Apps**" to customize the applications that can send notifications or the ones you wish not to send alerts during focus mode.
- Next up, choose "**Options**," then selected from the displayed options.
- Select the "**Back**" button.

Share your Focus Status

When you share your focus status and someone who's not on your allowed list tries to reach you, your focus status will pop up in messages, informing them that you're busy.

- Launch the Settings app.
- Then hit "**Focus**."
- Next up, select "**Focus Status**."
- Proceed by toggling on "**Share Focus Status**."
- Go ahead and choose the Focus mode (Personal, Driving, Work, etc.) you'll be sharing your status from.

Allow Calls from Emergency Contacts

You can let your emergency contacts bypass the focus mode restriction when they try to contact you.

- Launch the Contacts app.
- Then choose a contact.
- Next up, hit "**Edit**."
- After that, choose "**Text Tone**" or "**Ringtone**."
- Proceed by toggling on "**Emergency Bypass**."

Sync your Focus settings

If you use other Apple devices that runs on the same Apple ID, you can sync your focus settings across them.

- Launch the Settings app.
- Next up, hit "**Focus**."
- Hit on the toggle next to "**Share Across Devices**."

Add a Custom Focus

When you get to the Focus menu in the Settings app you don't fancy any of the preloaded Focus modes, you can create a custom version.

- Launch the Settings app.
- Next up, hit "**Focus**."
- Then select the plus icon in the upper right.
- After that, choose "**Custom**."
- Proceed by inserting a name for the Focus mode, press **Return**.
- Go ahead and pick a color.
- Then select an an icon for your Focus.
- Hit on "**Next**."
- Proceed by tapping the "**People**" tab, then select "**Allow Notifications**" to allow or "**Silence Notifications**" to mute notifications from the selected contacts. Do the same for the "**Apps**" tab.

Remove a Focus

- Launch the Settings app.
- After that, hit "**Focus**."
- Go ahead and select the Focus.
- Move to the bottom, then hit "**Delete Focus**."

Chapter Nineteen

How to use the Camera App

The Camera app enables users to capture amazing moments and also shoot high-definition videos and movies.

Capture a Photo
- Launch the Camera app.
- To start a timer before capturing, steady your iPad, then position the capture and select ⏱, then hit "**10s**" or "**3s**."
- Then select the Shutter button.
- To view the capture image, hit the Thumbnail icon. Or navigate to the Photos app.

Turn on the Camera Flash
- Launch the Camera app.
- Then choose the Flash button ⚡ at the top.
- Proceed by choosing your desired option: "**On**," **Auto**," or "**Off**."

Zoom in or out
- Launch the Camera app.
- Proceed by pinching in to zoom out, or out to zoom in.

Capture a Panorama Image
- Launch the Camera app.
- Swipe towards the left to switch to "**Pano**" mode.
- Then press the arrow icon to customize the capture direction.
- Then press the shutter icon to capture a panoramic image.
- Tilt your iPad to capture your environment. Ensure the arrow aligns with the yellow line.
- Press the shutter icon once more to cancel the panorama recording.

Capture a Live Photo
- Launch the Camera app.
- Then press the rings button at the top center to alternate to yellow color.
- Next up, press the Shutter icon to capture.

Capture with Burst mode

Burst mode allows users to capture several fast-moving images, giving them many images to choose from.

- Launch the Camera app.
- Then select "**Photo**" mode. Also, you can swipe to the "**Square**" mode.
- Long-tap the Shutter icon to swiftly capture plenty of images. The number of captured shots will be shown by the counter.
- Raise your finger to discontinue.
- To choose the images to keep, select the Burst thumbnail, then press "**Select**."
- Proceed by tapping the circle at the lower-right edge of the individual image you want to save.
- Then choose "**Done**."
- To erase the whole set of Burst images, select the thumbnail, then hit on the Delete icon.

Take a Selfie

- Launch the Camera app.
- Toggle on the front camera by pressing ⟳ or ⟲.
- Position your iPad on your face.
- Then hit the Shutter icon.

Mirror your Front Camera

Turning on mirror front camera, let you captured a mirrored selfie that appears the way it shows within the camera pane.

- Launch the Settings app.
- Next, select "**Camera**."
- Proceed by enabling "**Mirror Front Camera**."

Scan QR Code with Camera

With the Camera app, you can scan QR codes on your iPad. It can likewise be done with the Code Scanner.

- Launch the Camera app.
- Proceed by positioning the iPad to make the code shows up on the screen.
- Hit on the notification that pops up on the display to move to the applicable app or webpage.

Scan QR Code with Code Scanner

- Launch the Settings app.
- Then press "Control Center."
- Hit the plus icon beside the "**Code Scanner**" option.
- Visit the Control Center, then press the Code Scanner and lift your iPad so allow the code show up on the display.

Capture a selfie in Portrait Mode

Images captured in Portrait mode are sharper with an elegant blurred background.

- Launch the Camera app.
- Swipe to "**Portrait**" mode.
- Position your iPad on your face so that you appear within the portrait box.
- Select the Shutter icon to capture.

Adjust the Portrait Lighting Effect

Portrait Lighting let you apply studio level effect on your selfies captured in Portrait mode.

- Launch the Camera app.
- Swipe to "**Portrait**" mode.
- Go ahead and place your iPad on your face so that you appear within the portrait box.
- Proceed by dragging the Portrait Lighting button .
- Then pick a lighting effect; Stage Light, Natural Light, Studio Light, etc.
- After that, select the Shutter icon to capture the image.

Change Depth Control for Portrait Mode Selfies

You can adjust how blurry the background will be when capture in Portrait mode.

- Launch the Camera app.
- Switch to "**Portrait**" mode.
- Place your iPad on your face so that you appear within the portrait box.
- Then choose ƒ towards the right section of the display.
- Proceed by dragging the slider upward or downward to change the effect.
- Then select the Shutter icon to capture.

Capture in Slow-motion

- Launch the Camera app.
- Then select the flip icon to adjust to the front camera.
- Swipe left to choose the "**Slo-mo**" mode.
- Next up, select the shutter button.

Shoot a Time-Lapse Video

- Launch the Camera app.
- Switch to the "**Time-lapse**" mode.
- Proceed by setting your iPad to the point you wish to capture.

- Then select the Record icon. Select it once more to discontinue recording.

Save Camera Settings

You can set your camera to retain the last camera mode you used to capture a shot.

- Launch the Settings app.
- Hit on "**Camera**."
- Next up, select "**Preserve Settings**."

Enable Photo Grid

By making grid display when capturing an image, it can let you straighten and properly set your shot.

- Launch the Settings app.
- Next up, hit "**Camera**."
- Proceed by toggling on "**Grid**."

Change the Focus & Exposure

Although the iPad automatically adjusts the focus and exposure, you can manually do it.

- Press the display to show the automatic focus and exposure menu.
- Click the place you intend to reposition the focus area.

- Proceed by dragging the Exposure icon ☼ upward or downward to change the exposure. It is beside the focus area.
- You can save the current manual focus and exposure configuration for subsequent capture by long-tapping the focus area. When done, you'll see the "**AE/AF Lock**"; press the display to unlock the configuration.

Personalize your Cinematic Mode Videos

Cinematic mode works like Portrait mode; it blurs the surroundings of an image or video you're capturing while making the focus area sharper.

Disable the Cinematic effect

- Launch the Photos app.
- Navigate to a video that was captured using Cinematic mode.
- Hit on "**Edit**."
- Next up, select "**Cinematic**" from the upper menu of the display.
- After that, choose "**Done**."

- Follow the proceed to enable Cinematic mode.

Adjust the Focus Subject in a Cinematic Video

When shooting in Cinematic mode, the camera is able to detect subjects and figure out where to focus automatically.

- Launch the Photos app.
- Navigate to a video that was captured using Cinematic mode.
- Next up, press "**Edit**."
- Proceed by playing the video to the spot you intend to adjust the focus.
- Go ahead and press the new subject that is marked in yellow. To adjust the focus; press twice to add automatic focus scanning on the subject.
- Then choose "**Done**."

Change the Cinematic mode Depth of Field

- Launch the Photos app.
- Head to the video that was captured using Cinematic mode.
- From there, hit "**Edit**."
- Next up, hit 🅕.

- Proceed by dragging the slider that shows up horizontally to modify the depth.
- Next, choose "**Done**."

Take a Screen Recording

Thanks to the iPad built-in recorder, you can screen record when you wish.

- Launch the Settings app.
- Next up, hit "**Control Center**."
- Proceed by tapping the plus icon beside the "**Screen Recording**" option.
- Visit the Control Center menu by swiping downward from the top right.
- Select .
- Hold on for the three second timer to finish.
- To discontinue recording, press the red status bar at the upper area of the display, then press "**Stop**."
- The recorded video will be stored in the Photos app.

Take a Screenshot

Long-tap the top button and any of the volume button simultaneously. A thumbnail will popover at the bottom left corner, click it to access the screenshot. The screenshot will be stored in the Photos app.

Chapter Twenty

How to use Live Text

With Live Text, users can quickly discover more about an image or text, including other types of media, through the internet.

Enable Live Text

To start, ensure that Live Text is enabled on your iPad.

- Launch the Settings app.
- Next up, choose "**General**."
- After that, hit "**Language & Region**."
- Proceed by turning on the "**Live Text**" toggle to green.

Use Live Text with Camera

The Camera app is able to detect texts and other media content that appear in the camera frame and offers a variety of ways to interact with them. This allows you to choose the text to translate, copy, and carry out other actions, such as phone calls. You can also use Live Text across different apps.

- Launch the Camera.

- Then set your iPad to make sure that the texts show up within the camera window.
- Then select the Live Text icon.
- Long-tap the text, then drag the selector tool to choose the particular text.
- Choose "Translate," "Select All," "Copy Text," etc., to perform your desired action.
- Then choose the Live Text icon to go back to Camera.

Disable Live Text for Camera

- Launch the Settings app.
- Then choose "**Camera**."
- Proceed by hitting the toggle next to "**Show Detected Text**" to deactivate it.

Translate, Copy and Look Up Text in an Image or Video

- Navigate to an image or pause a movie that has text.
- Then select the Detect Text icon.
- Long-tap the chosen text.
- Proceed by dragging the selector tool to choose a particular specific text.

- Then choose any of the options: Share, Translate, Look Up, etc.

- Then choose the Detect Text icon to go back to the image or movie.

Perform Tasks on an Image or Video

Based on the content, users can press a quick option at the bottom of the window to perform actions like translate text, make phone calls, etc.

- Navigate to the Photos app and open up an image that has a text.

- Then choose the Detect Text icon

- Proceed by tapping a quick action from the bottom of the window.

- Next up, hit the Detect Text icon to go back to the image/video.

Identify Objects with Visual Look Up

Visual Look Up will let you discover more about plants, landmarks, animals and other important landscape and structures in an image or video.

- Start by opening an image in full screen. To look up a video, simply pause it.
- Then, select the star icon such as ![icon] or ![icon] if it appears.
- Next up, hit "**Look Up**" on the upper menu of the image detail.
- To exit, press outside the result, then select the Close icon.

How to use the Document Scanner

Apple has included a document scanner in the iPad that enables users to quickly scan their files.

Scan a Document
- Launch the Notes app.
- Then choose the pen and note sign.

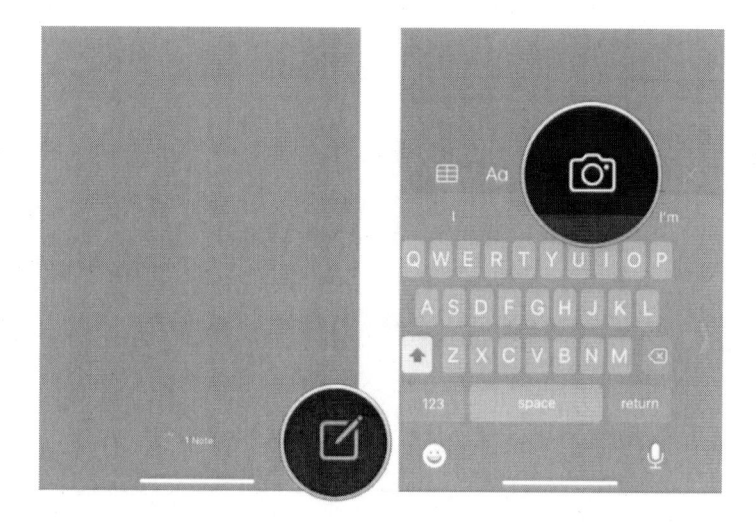

- Then hit on the camera icon.
- Next up, choose "**Scan Documents**."
- Position the paper you want to scan, then hit the shutter button if the scanning doesn't start automatically.
- Then choose "**Save**."
- You can access the scanned copy in the Notes app.

Share the Scanned Document

- Start by selecting the scanned document.
- Then press the share button in the upper-right corner.
- Choose the app through which you desire to share the note.
- Follow the prompts to share.

Remove a Scanned Document
- Choose the file you intend to share.
- Next up, choose the trash can icon in the lower-right corner.
- Then choose "**Delete Scan**."

Chapter Twenty-One

How to use Find My App

With the Find My app, you can track the location of someone, including your misplaced Apple devices, and even lock and delete content remotely, erase, and locate misplaced Apple devices. You can also set the app to always share your current location and more.

Adding iPad to Find My

To ensure you can track your misplaced iPad when it gets lost, you'll have to link the iPad to your Apple ID.

- Launch the Settings app.
- Then select your name at the top.
- Hit on "**Find My**."
- When prompted, log in and input your Apple ID.
- Then go through the instructions.
- Hit on "**Find My iPad**."
- Proceed by turning on "**Find My iPad**."

Add Friends

You can choose the people or contacts who can see your locations and duration.

- Launch the Find My app.

- Then hit the "**People**" tab from the bottom.
- Next up, choose "**Share My Location**."
- Input the name or email of the person with whom you desire to share your location. Choose the plus button to include more people.
- Then choose how long you'd like to share your location.

Locate your Friends

People can share their location with you, and you can view the details.

- Launch the Find My app.
- Then hit the "**People**" tab from the bottom.
- Go ahead and choose the person who shared their location with you.

Share your Location

You can choose to enable or disable location sharing at any time.

- Launch the Find My app.
- Hit the "**Me**" tab at the bottom.
- Proceed by hitting the toggle beside the "**Share My Location**."

Receive Alerts when your Friend Arrives or Exits a Location

- Launch the Find My app.
- From the lower left, hit the "**People**" tab.
- Proceed by tapping the person's name you intend to get notification on.
- Underneath "**Notifications**," hit "**Add**."
- Next up, choose "**Notify Me**."
- Go ahead and select to get notification whenever your pal enters or exits a location.
- Next up, select a location, or hit "**New Location**" to insert a new location including its perimeter.
- Proceed by selecting to get notification just once or every time.
- Then choose "**Add**."
- Now, select "**OK**."
- Your pal will receive a notification once you're done setting the notification.
- However, for recurring notification, your pal will need to authorize it before it's turned on. They'll receive a notification asking for permission whenever they enter at or exit the selected location.

Receive Alert when your Friend is not at a Location

You can set your iPad to get notification if your relative or pal is not at a particular location at a given time.

- Launch the Find My app.
- From the lower left, hit the "**People**" tab.
- Proceed by tapping the contact you wish to get notification about.
- Underneath "**Notifications**," hit "**Add**."
- Next up, select "**Notify Me**."
- Underneath the "**When**" header, hit on "**[your pal's name] Is Not At**."
- Go ahead and select a location, or hit on "New Location" to enter a new location information.
- Choose when to get notified by tapping the "**Time**" and "**Days**" tab to make a selection.
- Then choose "**Add**."
- After that, select "**OK**."
- Your pal will receive a notification asking for permission before it's enabled.

Manage your Notification

- Launch the Find My app.

- From the lower left, hit the "**People**" tab.
- Go ahead and choose the person's name that you intend to adjust or disable their notification.
- Underneath "**Notifications**," hit the notification.
- Then select "**Change a notification**" to adjust any information, then choose "**Done**." Or hit "**Turn off a notification**," then choose "**Delete Notification**," and select "**Delete Notification**" once more.

Alert a friend when you Change Location

- Launch the Find My app.
- From the lower left, hit the "**People**" tab.
- Go ahead and choose the person you intend to notify.
- Then underneath "**Notifications**," hit "**Add**."
- Next up, select "**Notify [your friend's name]**."
- Proceed by selecting if you wish to alert your pal when you enter or exit a location.
- Go ahead and select a location, or hit "**New Location**" to add a new location, then set its perimeter.

- Go ahead and select if your pal should be notified just once or every time.
- Then choose "**Add**."

View all your Notifications
- Launch the Find My app.
- Hit on the "**Me**" tab in the lower-left.
- Underneath the "**Notifications About You**" header, you'll see the persons that are alerted about your change in location.
- Click on a name to view additional information.

Disable Notifications about you
You disable your location-based notifications, including the ones you made yourself and the ones created by your friends.

- Launch the Find My app.
- Hit on the "**Me**" tab in the lower-left.
- Underneath the "**Notifications About You**" header, you'll see the persons that are alerted about your change in location.
- Then choose a name.
- Next up, click on a notification.
- After that, hit "**Delete Notification**."

- Hit on "**Delete Notification**" once more.

Locate Devices

If you misplaced your Apple device, the Find My app can help you locate it.

- Launch the Find My app.
- Then choose the "**Devices**" tab from the bottom.
- Go ahead and choose the device you desire to locate.
- If it can be tracked, the device will open up on a map. Otherwise, you'll see "No location found." However, if it does appear on the map, you can hit the "**Play Sound**" to make it ring.
- Press "**Directions**" to load the map of the device's location.

Find Lost Devices

If you can't track the lost device, you can mark it as lost and secure it with a passcode. In this manner, even if it turns up, no one can access it. Your phone number will display on the device so that when it is eventually found by someone else, they can dial it.

- Launch the Find My app.
- Then choose the "**Devices**" tab on the bottom.
- Next up, choose "**Mark As Lost**."

- Then hit "**Activate**."
- After this, hit "**Continue**."
- Go ahead and input a passcode.
- Proceed by writing a memo that will appear on the lost device.
- Then choose "**Activate**" or "**Lock**."

Erase a Device

Also, you can wipe a device clean if it can't be tracked.

- Launch the Find My app.
- Then choose the "**Devices**" tab on the bottom.
- Then choose the device.
- Next up, select "**Erase This Device**."
- After that, choose "**Continue**."
- Follow the prompts.

Chapter Twenty-Two

How to use Apple Freeform App

The Freeform application fosters collaboration. Users can write, sketch, and design on it. You can even import stickers, PDFs, images, videos, links, and much more.

Create a Freeform board

You can utilize the Freeform application to generate boards for formulation of ideas and collaboration.

Create a new board

- Launch the Freeform app.
- Then select the pen and paper icon .
- Then choose an option from the icons show at the upper section of the display. For text box, choose . For sticky note, hit to begin creating your board.

- You can navigate over the board by clenching your finger. Pinch your fingers close or wide to zoom in/out. To accurately enlarge it, press the percentage at the lower-left edge.
- To title the board, hit on "**Untitled**" at the upper left, then choose "**Rename**."

Create a board using another app

Interestingly, users can begin afresh a Freeform board with items from other supported applications, like Photos, Notes, Files, etc.

- Launch the supported app and navigate to the content you intend to share.
- Then select Share or .
- After that, hit on .
- Next up, choose "**New Board**." Alternatively, you can select the title of an old board.

Open a board

- Launch the Freeform app.
- Proceed by selecting a category from the sidebar.
- Next up, select the board you intend to view. If the sidebar doesn't appear, hit ▭. However, if you are already in a board, hit the Back button at the top left edge.
- Hit on ▦ for grid view or ☰ for list view.
- To filter the boards by name rather than by recently updated, hit ▦ or ☰, then select "**Sort by Name**."
- If you need to include a board to Favorites when surfing through the "All Boards" menu, long-tap the board title or its thumbnail, then press ♡. However, if you are already in a board

and intend to favorite it, press ⌵ , then click ♡ .

Duplicate a board
- When on the "**All Boards**" menu, choose "**Select**" from the upper-right edge. Proceed by tapping the boards you intend to copy. After that, choose "**Duplicate**." Alternatively, long-tap the thumbnail of the board, and hit "**Duplicate**."
- However, if you are in a board, select ⌵ , then choose "**Duplicate**."

Add and Format Shapes
Users can include diagrams, shapes and lines to a board.

- Launch the Freeform app.

- Navigate to a board, or press ✎ to begin afresh.

- Then select ▢.
- Proceed by choosing an arrow, shape or line to have it added to the board.
- Click to choose the shape/line and display its formatting tools.
- Hit on ● to adjust its color.
- Choose ╱ to adjust the line design, then select the stroke color and thickness.
- Hit on ↗ to sap the lines to arrows.
- However, if you choose connection line, choose ↳ to adjust it to curvy, straight or corner.
- To adjust the shape type, hit ⋯, then choose "**Change Shape**," and select a different shape.

Create a diagram

Creating flowcharts in the Freeform app is easy thanks to the use of connectors and shape selector.

- Launch the Freeform app.

119

- Navigate to a board, or press ✎ to begin afresh.
- From the lower right edge of the window, choose ⌒ (if you're in full screen). However, if you're in split view, choose ▦, then select **"Show Connectors."**
- Draw your diagram by clicking an icon at the center top.
-
- Proceed by dragging a connector arrow to the position you prefer to have the next part of the diagram. A little menu will show up; go ahead and choose the next shape you intend to include.

Draw or Handwrite

While in the Freeform application, users can draw and compose handwritten notes using an Apple Pencil.

- Launch the Freeform app.

- Navigate to a board, or press ▣ to begin afresh.

- Then hit Ⓐ .
- Proceed by drawing with your finger or use the Apple Pencil.
- If you are currently sketching with an Apple Pencil, but wish to switch to drawing with your fingers, then choose ⓘ , and select "**Draw with Finger**."
- Click on a tool to start using it or swipe to view other tools.
- Double-tap a tool to adjust its opacity or thickness.

Choose Items & Scroll using Apple Pencil

While using the Freeform application, your Apple Pencil only functions to write and sketch, but you can adjust it to choose items and scroll.

- Launch the Settings app.
- Then choose "Freeform."
- Proceed by toggling on "**Select and Scroll**" under "**Apple Pencil**."

- Once you've changed the setting, select ⒶA from the toolbox to sketch. Hit on the icon once more select and scroll using Apple Pencil.

Chapter Twenty-Three

How to use the Reminders App

If you're forgetful, then the Reminder app can help you track important dates and times so that you don't miss the events on those selected days.

Add a Reminders
- Launch the Reminders app.
- Then select "**+ New Reminder**."
- Proceed by inputting your task.

Add a Scheduled Reminder
You can add an upcoming event that you want to be reminded a specific time.

- Launch the Reminders app.
- Next up, select "**+ New Reminder**" button.
- Now, press the "*i*" icon.
- Proceed by inputting your task.
- Go ahead and hit the toggle beside "**Remind me on a day**."

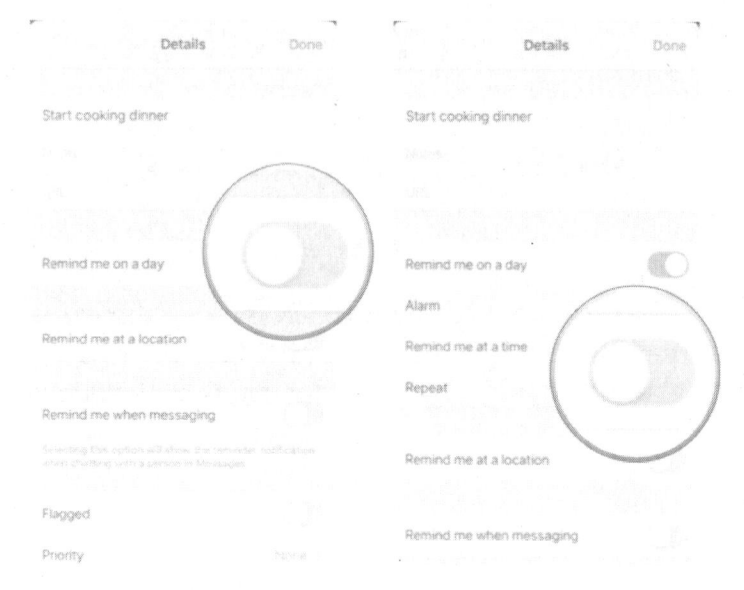

- Also, hit the toggle beside "**Remind me at a time**" to enable it.
- Then choose "**Alarm**."
- Proceed by selecting your preferred date and time.
- After that, choose "**Done**."

Add a Repeating Scheduled Reminder

- Launch the Reminders app.
- After this, press the "+ **New Reminder**" button.
- Then select the "*i*" icon.
- Go ahead and insert your task.
- Hit the toggle beside "**Remind me on a day**" to enable it.

- Hit the toggle beside "**Remind me at a time**" to activate it.
- Then select "**Alarm**."
- Proceed by choosing the date and time.
- Then choose "**Repeat**."
- Choose how often you want the reminder to repeat. Or select "**Custom**" to personalize it.
- Choose **"End Repeat"** to specify when you'd like the reminder to stop.
- To keep the reminder running indefinitely, select "**Repeat Forever**."
- Lastly, choose "**Done**."

Add a Location-Based Reminder

You can configure the app to notify you of something before you reach or exit a specific location.

- Launch the Reminders app.
- After this, press the "**+ New Reminder**" button.
- Then select the "***i***" icon.
- Go ahead and insert your task.
- Hit on the toggle beside "**Remind me at a location**."

- Then choose "**Location**."
- Proceed by selection your preferred location.
- Then press "**Arriving**" or "**Leaving**."
- Go ahead and drag the the black icon to adjust the radius where you wish to get the notification.
- Then choose "**Done**."

Chapter Twenty-Four

How to use Tab Groups in Safari

Tab groups enables users to organize related URLS or links for easy access.

Create a Tab Group
- Launch the Safari app.
- Next up, press the tab icon on the lower right corner.

- Proceed by tapping the "X Tabs" in center. X refers to the number of tabs.

- Next up, hit on "**New Empty Tab Group.**"

- Go ahead and insert a group name for the tab.
- Lastly, select "**Save**."

Reorder Safari Tab Groups
- Launch the Safari app.
- Next up, press the tab icon on the lower right corner.
- Proceed by tapping the tab group title in the center (for example "**News**)".

- Then choose "**Edit**" from the upper left.
- Long-tap the three lines next to the tab group.
- Then move the tab to your preferred position.
- Now, select "**Done**."

Transfer a Tab to a different Tab Group
- Launch the Safari app.
- Next up, select the tab icon.
- Then select the "**Move to Tab Group**" button.
- Proceed by choosing the tab you desire to add to the group.

Rename a Tab Group
- Launch the Safari app.
- Long-press the tab group name.
- Then choose "**Rename**."
- Proceed by inputting a new name.
- After that, choose "**Save**."

Close All Tab Group
- Launch the Safari app.
- Long-tap the tabs button at the lower right.
- Next up, choose "**Close All X Tabs**."

Remove a Safari Tab Group

- Launch the Safari app.
- Then select the tabs button.
- Proceed by tapping the group name of the tab at the lower menu.
- Then long-tap the desired tab group.
- Then choose "**Delete**."

How to use Extensions on Safari

You can personalize the Safari browser by installing extensions in the app. For instance, certain extensions can help you correct grammatical errors when typing, discover coupons and offers while shopping online, and so on.

Install Safari extensions

- Launch the Safari app.
- Hit on the Manage Extensions icon . It is positioned to the right of the search box.

- Next up, choose "**Manage Extensions**."
- After that, hit "**More Extensions**" to explore the App Store for additional extensions.
- Once you've located your preferred extension, click the price if it's premium, or select "**Get**" if its free.
- Follow the prompts.

Manage your Extensions

You can control which extension you wish to turn on or off.

- Launch the Safari app.
- Hit on the Manage Extensions icon ⌧. It is positioned to the right of the search box.
- After that, choose "**Manage Extensions**."
- Proceed by selecting or deselecting an extension's checkbox to enable or disable it.

Use Extensions

Extension are used to extend your browser functionality or to adjust how your browser works.

- Launch the Safari browser.

- Then choose the Manage Extensions icon ⊡.
- Next up, select "**Manage Extensions**."
- Proceed by tapping the extension you desire to grant permissions to.
- Go through the prompts to select the level of access to grant the extension.

Change Extension Settings

You can switch on or off an extension for a particular website only.

- Launch the Safari app.
- Next up, press the Manage Extensions icon ⊡.
- Then select "**Manage Extensions**."
- Proceed by turning on or off the extension.

Delete an Extension

- Start by swiping downward on your home screen.
- Go ahead and search for the extension you intend to delete.
- Long-tap the extension icon.
- Next up, choose "**Delete app**."
- Follow the prompts.

Remove Ads & Distractions in Safari

When you turn on the Safari Reader while browsing with the Safari app, it will allow you to view the website without showing the menu, advertisements, or anything else that can distract you, thereby only letting you see the relevant text and photos.

Show Reader

- Hit on the Page Settings icon AA. It is positioned to the left side of the search box.
- Next up, choose "**Show Reader.**"
- To go back to the full page, hit on the Page Settings icon AA, then choose "**Hide Reader.**"

Enable Reader Automatically

- Launch the Safari app.
- Navigate to a website.
- Hit the Page Settings icon AA.

- Next up, choose "Website Settings."
- Proceed by turning on "**Use Reader Automatically**."

Block pop-ups
- Launch the Settings app.
- Then choose "**Safari**.
- Proceed by toggling on "**Block Pop-ups**."

Chapter Twenty-Five

How to use the Weather App

The Weather app enables users to see the weather conditions of their location and other places, including the option to manage weather notifications and more.

Check the weather

The Weather application makes tracking the weather condition, weather forecast, and information about your current location and other places on the iPad easy.

Enable Location Services

Ensure you enable location services so that you get accurate weather information.

- Launch the Settings app.
- Next up, hit "**Privacy & Security**."
- After that, select "**Location Services**."
- Hit on "**Weather**."
- Proceed by toggling on "**Precise Location**."

Check the Local Forecast

- Once you launch the Weather app, it should show your weather information for your current location. However, if it doesn't, press the Show Sidebar icon ▣ , then hit on "**My Location**."
- Simply swipe up to see weather information such as severe weather alerts, Air quality, 10-day forecast and more.

Personalize the Weather Units

The US uses Fahrenheit, while most countries are okay with using Celsius for their weather data. The same applies to other units of measurement, such as miles per hour, knots, etc.

- Launch the Weather app.
- Then choose the Sidebar icon ▣. Alternatively, you can flip your iPad to landscape orientation to show the sidebar.
- Then select ⬤ .
- After that, choose "**Units**."
- Proceed by selecting the weather information that you desire to change its measurement unit. For temperature,

select "**Change temperature units,**" then hit on "**Celsius**" or "**Fahrenheit**."

Change the location shown in the Weather widget

Weather widgets provides a quick glance at the weather conditions and predictions right on the home screen.

You can adjust the location that appears on the weather widget.

- Long-tap the Weather widget on the home screen.
- Then choose "**Edit widget**."
- Next up, select "**My Location**."
- Go ahead and select the location you wish to show up in the widget.

View the weather in another Location

Aside from checking the weather in your current location, you can also track the weather in places you plan to visit.

- Launch the Weather app.
- Then choose the Sidebar icon .
- Proceed by tapping the search box at the upper menu of the display, then input a location.

- Go ahead and select the location from the search results to see the weather prediction.
- Select "**Cancel**" to exit the forecast.

Add a Location to your weather list

If you have other locations where you want to always see their weather forecast, you can include them in your weather list.

- Launch the Weather app.
- Then choose the Sidebar icon.
- Proceed by tapping the search box at the upper menu of the display, then input a location.
- Go ahead and select the location from the search results.
- Then select "**Add**."
- To swiftly see the weather in the added location(s), press the Sidebar icon, then choose the location.

Remove a Location in your weather list

- Launch the Weather app.
- Then choose the Sidebar icon.

- Proceed by swiping leftward on the location.

- Then select 🗑.

Reorder Locations in your weather list
- Long-tap the location.
- Then drag it upward or downward.

Enable Weather Notifications
- Launch the Settings app.
- Next up, select "**Privacy & Security**."
- From there, choose "**Location Services**."
- Now, select "**Weather**."
- Hit on "**Always**."
- Ensure you've turned on "**Precise Location**" to get the updated and accurate alert for your current location.
- Launch the Weather app.
- Then choose the Sidebar icon.
- Then select.
- Hit on "**Notifications**."
- Proceed by authorizing notifications from the app.

- Proceed by turning on alert for **"Severe Weather"** and other data underneath the **"Current Location"** header.
- Next up, select **"Done."**

Chapter Twenty-Six

Disable Location-Based Suggestions

- Launch the Settings app.
- Next up, choose "**Privacy & Security**."
- After that, hit "**Location Services**."
- Hit on "**System Services**."
- Proceed by toggling off "**Suggestions & Search**."

Lock/Unlock the Screen Orientation

Some applications appear differently whenever you rotate the iPad. However, you can freeze the screen orientation from changing whoever you flip the iPad.

- Navigate to the Control Center, then press the Lock Orientation icon .

Add a Dictionary

You can add the dictionary that you intend to use in searches.

- Launch the Settings app.
- Next up, choose "**General**."
- After that, hit "**Dictionary**."
- Then choose a dictionary.

View the Battery Percentage

You can make the battery percentage to display in the status bar.

- Launch the Settings app.
- Then choose "**Battery**."
- Proceed by toggling on "**Battery Percentage**."

Reduce Loud Headphone Sound

- Launch the Settings app.
- Then select "**Sounds**."

- Hit on "**Headphone Safety**."
- Go ahead and press the toggle next to "**Reduce Loud Sounds**."
- Proceed by dragging the slider to your desired maximum volume.

Schedule Downtime

Sometimes you may decide stay away from your iPad. You can disable alerts, messages, and calls from coming in. However, you can authorize calls from certain people if you wish.

- Launch the Settings app.
- Next up, hit "**Screen Time**."
- After that, hit "**App & Website Activity**." Toggle it on.
- Now, select "**Downtime**."
- Hit on "**Scheduled**."
- From there, hit "**Customize Days**" or "**Every Day**."
- Go ahead and input the start and end times.

Add App Limits

You can add a duration that you don't want to exceed when using certain applications.

- Launch the Settings app.
- Then, hit "**Screen Time**."
- Hit on "**App Limits**."
- Next up, press "**Add Limit**."
- Proceed by selecting your desired app category.
- Then choose the app.
- Now, select "**Next**."
- Proceed by adding the duration allowed.
- If you need to input a duration for each day, hit on "**Customize Days**.", then add the limits for the particular days.
- Next up, choose "**Add**."

Enable Dark Mode

Dark Mode offers a dark theme that doesn't strain the eyes when using your tablet.

- Launch the Settings app.
- Hit on "**Display & Brightness**."
- Next up, choose "**Dark**."

Enable True Tone

Once enabled, True Tone will automatically adjust the screen's brightness and color temperature to correspond with the ambient light.

- Launch the Settings app.
- Hit on "**Display & Brightness**."
- Proceed by toggling on "**True Tone**."

Add Notification Summary

Notification summaries help users cut down on the number of messages they get during a specific time. So, rather than getting them randomly, users can schedule the particular time they desire to get all received notifications displayed on their iPad.

- Launch the Settings app.
- Then select "**Notifications**."
- Afterward, hit "**Scheduled Summary**."
- Proceed by press the toggle beside the "**Scheduled Summary**" option to enable it.
- Next up, choose "**Continue**."
- Beneath the "**Apps in Summary**" submenu, go ahead and select the applications you desire to include in your Notification Summary.
- After this, press "**Add [no.] apps**,"
- Then set your schedule.

- Next up, select "**Add Summary**" to include additional Notification Summaries.
- Afterward, press "**Turn on Notification Summary**."

Adjust how Notifications Appear

- Launch the Settings app.
- Then choose "**Notifications**."
- Underneath the "**Display As**" section, go ahead and select "**List**," "**Count**" or "**Stack**" to set the pattern you prefer your notifications to be displayed on the Lock Screen.

Adjust Alert Styles

- Launch the Settings app.
- Then hit "**Notifications**."
- Proceed by choosing an application underneath "**Notification Style**."
- Go ahead and select your desired alert style underneath "**Alerts**."
- Ensure you enable "**Allow Notifications**," then select the

duration you desire for the notifications to be sent.

Adjust Group Notification Settings

- Launch the Settings app.
- Then hit "**Notifications**."
- Proceed by choosing an application.
- Next up, select "**Notification Grouping**."
- Go ahead and hit on "**By App**," "**Automatic**" or "**Off**."

Disable Notifications for Apps

- Launch the Settings app.
- Then hit "**Notifications**."
- Next up, hit "**Siri Suggestions**."
- Proceed by turning off any application.

Adjust Notifications Appearance on Lock Screen

- Launch the Settings app.
- Next up, select "**Notifications**."
- Go ahead and hit on an application.
- After this, select "**Show Previews**."
- Then hit on an option.

Create a Memoji

Users can conveniently create memoji to suit their personality or mimic their current feeling.

Add a Memoji

- Launch the Messages app.
- Go ahead and hit the Compose icon or head over to a previous chat.
- Then hit the plus icon.
- Swipe upward, then hit the Memoji button.

- Proceed by swiping right, then hit "**New Memoji**."
- Proceed by customizing the bros, hairstyles, eyes, nose, etc.
- Afterward, choose "**Done**."

Edit a Memoji
- Launch the Messages application.
- Navigate and press the Memoji icon.
- Go ahead and select the Memoji you desire to customize.
- Hit on the triple dots at the lower-left of the Memoji.
- Next up, choose "**Edit**."

Edit

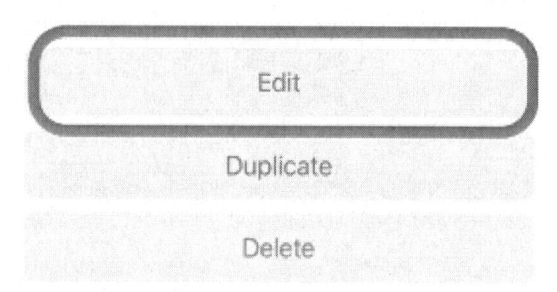

Duplicate

Delete

Conclusion

The iPad Air 2024 outperforms its predecessor, the 2022 model, thanks to offering two screen sizes and the addition of the M2 chip, which enhances AI capabilities. Also, it outperforms the older model thanks to its storage capacity, RAM size, and 10-core GPU. It is a bridge between lower iPads and the iPad Pro 2024, but nonetheless, the iPad Air offers users access to a budget-friendly flagship device.

About the Author

Shawn Blaine is a gadget reviewer, programmer, and computer geek.

Growing up, he loved playing video games and had special affection for robots. As a teenager, he learned Arduino and built several real-world projects, such as a GPS tracker, a digital pet, a light controller, and more. He soon developed a love for tech journalism, which inspired him to write books on new products such as the iPhone, Samsung, Google Pixel, etc.

He has previously worked for several large tech companies. He's currently focused on coding and blockchain development but still finds time to write and teach people how to use their smartphones, PCs, and other devices.

Index

A

Add a Dictionary 13, 142
AirDrop 5, 6, 41, 42, 43
Alert Styles...14, 146
App Limits ..14, 143, 144
Apple Cash.4, 16, 18
Apple Freeform App........... 12, 115
Apple Pay... 3, 4, 14, 15, 16, 19, 20
Apple Pencil5, 12, 2, 38, 39, 40, 68, 120, 121, 122

B

Backup your iPad 3, 11
Battery Percentage 14, 142
Burst mode 9, 92

C

Calendars.. 5, 32, 33
Camera App....9, 90
Camera Flash..9, 90
Cellular Service. 3, 5
Center Stage... 9, 84
Cinematic Mode.10, 97
Contacts5, 9, 32, 33, 41, 42, 88
Control Center6, 41, 44, 45, 46, 47, 52, 56, 67, 82, 84, 85, 93, 99, 141
Create a Memoji.14, 148
Create your Apple ID.................3, 10

D

Dark Mode .. 14, 144
Depth Control10, 95
Downtime.... 14, 143

E

eSIM 3, 5

F

FaceTime... 8, 9, 79, 80, 81, 82, 84, 85
Factory Reset ..3, 13
Family Sharing.... 4, 22, 23, 24
Find My App 11, 107
Focus Mode.... 9, 86

Folder........ 8, 76, 77
Front Camera 10, 93

G

Google Account.... 5, 32

H

Hide My Email..... 5, 34, 35, 36, 37
Home Screen 8, 60, 63, 64, 71, 74, 75, 76, 77, 78

I

Install New iPadOS 3, 8
Install Safari extensions 13, 130
iPad as Second Monitor 7, 67

L

Live Photo....... 9, 91
Live Text 10, 101, 102
Location-Based Suggestions 13, 141

M

Mail.... 5, 32, 33, 34, 62

N

Notification Settings..... 14, 147
Notification Summary 14, 145, 146

O

Open Apps........ 3, 6

P

Panorama Image. 9, 91
Passcode.... 4, 3, 25, 26, 27, 28, 30, 31
Photo Grid.... 10, 96
Picture in Picture .7, 58
Portrait Lighting Effect.......... 10, 94
Portrait Mode.9, 10, 82, 94, 95

Q

Quick Note 6, 48, 49, 50, 51

R

Reduce Loud Headphone Sound....... 14, 142
Reminders App ..12, 123

Reorder Apps.. 8, 74

S

Safari.12, 13, 49, 50, 127, 128, 129, 130, 131, 132, 133, 134
Scan a Document 11, 104
Scan QR Code 10, 93
Screen Orientation 13, 141
Screen Recording 10, 99
Set up iPad............ 3
SharePlay. 9, 80, 81, 82
Siri ... 7, 8, 4, 69, 70, 147
Slide Over 7, 60, 61, 62, 63
Slow-motion . 10, 95
Split View. 7, 62, 63, 64
Stage Manager. 6, 1, 52, 53, 56, 57

T

Tab Groups . 12, 127, 128

Take a Screenshot 10, 100
Take a Selfie ... 9, 92
Time-Lapse Video 10, 95
Touch ID 4, 2, 3, 20, 25, 26, 27, 28, 30, 31
True Tone... 14, 144, 145
Turn on your iPad 3, 4

U

Universal Control.7, 65, 66

V

Visual Look Up 11, 1, 104
Voice Isolation 9, 84

W

Weather App 13, 135
Wide Spectrum ... 9, 84
Widgets 8, 71, 72, 73

Manufactured by Amazon.ca
Acheson, AB